LINCOLN - MERCURY
DEALERS PRESENT
ED SULLIVAN AND HIS
TOAST OF THE TOWN

CBS TV STU

CBS

cORDial
RESTAURANT BAR

BAR
RESTAURANT

A REALLY BIG SHOW

A VISUAL HISTORY OF THE ED SULLIVAN SHOW

A REALLY BIG SHOW

TEXT BY JOHN LEONARD

EDITED BY CLAUDIA FALKENBURG AND ANDREW SOLT

ART DIRECTION BY LLOYD ZIFF

SARAH LAZIN BOOKS

VIKING
STUDIO
BOOKS

MARIANNE PARTRIDGE
Consulting Editor

GREG VINES
Associate Editor

TIMOTHY JONES
Lloyd Ziff Design Group, Inc.
Design Associate

MICK HAGGERTY
Chapter Illustrations

VIKING STUDIO BOOKS

Published by the Penguin Group
Viking Penguin, a division of Penguin Books USA Inc.,
375 Hudson Street, New York, New York 10014, U.S.A.
Penguin Books Ltd., 27 Wrights Lane,
London W8 5TZ, England
Penguin Books Australia Ltd., Ringwood,
Victoria, Australia
Penguin Books Canada Ltd., 10 Alcorn Avenue, Suite 300,
Toronto, Ontario, Canada M4V 3B2
Penguin Books (N.Z.) Ltd., 182–190 Wairau Road,
Auckland 10, New Zealand

Penguin Books Ltd., Registered Offices:
Harmondsworth, Middlesex, England

First published in 1992 by Viking Penguin,
a division of Penguin Books USA Inc.

1 3 5 7 9 10 8 6 4 2

LIBRARY OF CONGRESS CATALOGING IN PUBLICATION DATA
Leonard, John.
A really big show : a visual history of the Ed Sullivan show /
text by John Leonard : edited by Claudia Falkenburg and Andrew Solt.
p.   cm.
"Sarah Lazin Books."
ISBN 0–670–84246–X
1. Ed Sullivan show (Television program)—Pictorial works.
I. Falkenburg, Claudia.   II. Solt, Andrew.   III. Title.
PN1992.77.E35L46   1992
791.45'72   dc20   92—54067

Printed in the United States of America

Contents

 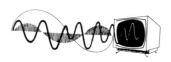

S UNDAY N IGHT, S EPTEMBER 11, 1966

This is just one

of the 1,087 hour-long shows that

America watched every Sunday night at 8 o'clock

from June 20, 1948, to May 30, 1971.

8:00

"Good evening, ladies and gentlemen. Tonight, from New York,

The Ed Sullivan Show. And now, launching his nineteenth season,

Ed Sullivan . . ."

8:01

"Good evening, ladies and gentlemen. Out here in our audience tonight there are a lot of youngsters. I'm sure some of them were not born when we started. This is the start of our nineteenth year. Now before you enjoy hilarious Red Skelton, Louis Armstrong, Robert Goulet, *Holiday on Ice* sensation Ronnie Robertson and thirty others of his skating cast . . . Right now we open tonight's show with the Rolling Stones' version of 'Paint It, Black,' and here they are."

8:04

"The Rolling Stones will be back later in the show singing 'Lady Jane' and 'Have You Seen Your Mother, Baby.'"

8:06

"I'm recalling that it was back in 1945 in Milwaukee that Morris Chalfin's *Holiday on Ice* made its debut. And for twenty years the spectacular attraction has played all over the world representing our country and has made so many friends. So let's have a wonderful hand for them as they come out."

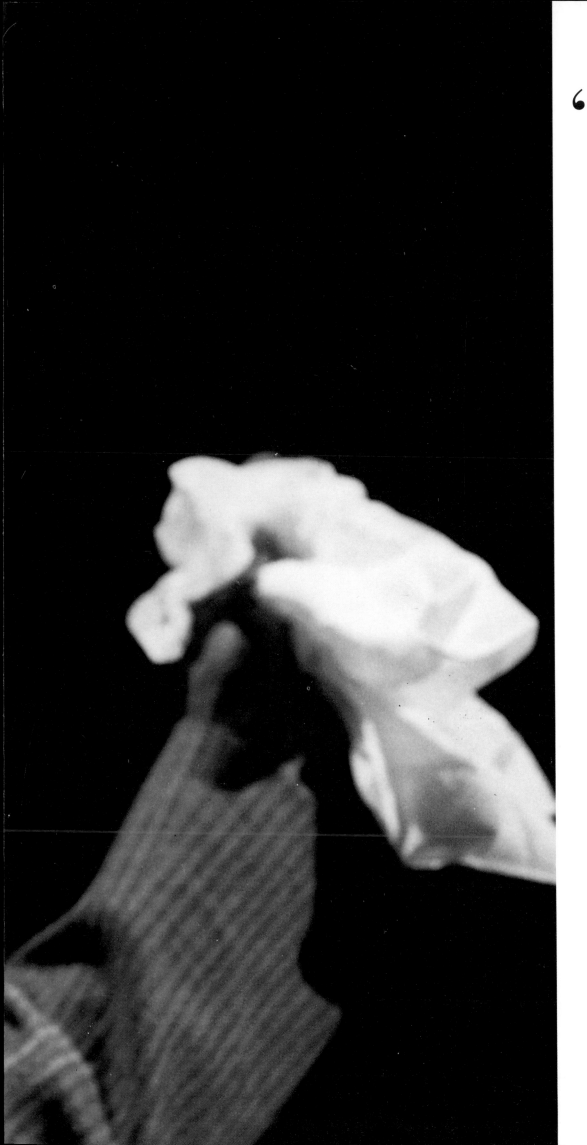

8:18

66 Here's a great American
who has represented our
country brilliantly and
winningly all over the
world — Louis 'Satchmo'
Armstrong. 99

8:22

"Now, here's a young comedienne, you've seen her on our stage before. She's simply delightful. Her name is Joan Rivers, and let's bring her on with a nice hand. Would you please."

8:28

"Years ago, years ago when Jack Lawrence recommended me as a sportswriter to the New York *Evening Mail* sports editor Sam Murphy — that was back in the 1920s — New York City had exactly sixteen daily newspapers, and today as you know, there are only four. But all of them headlined tonight's appearance of Robert Goulet. So ladies and gentlemen, here is Robert Goulet."

8:37

"Now, ladies and gentlemen, here is one of the kindliest stars that show business has ever produced — Red Skelton."

8:48

"The Rolling Stones. Go!"

8:55

"Now highlighting the show next Sunday night will be the appearance of an old friend of mine and yours, comedy star Jackie Mason. So, I want to call him out here. Jackie Mason! It's nice to have you back here on our stage. The newspapermen have been calling up about it. It's going to be a gala occasion, and it's great that you're coming back and come back often. Let's have a fine hand for Jackie Mason. Good night."

On the Air

To think that you're gonna be on television with Ed Sullivan was comparable to a nightclub comedian in those days to playing the epitome of a nightclub like the Copacabana. Or an opera singer being at the Met. Or, if a guy is an architect that makes the Empire State Building. This was the biggest.
—JACKIE MASON

Toast of the Town moved in 1949 to Studio 50, renamed for Sullivan himself in 1968, where all "live" CBS shows originated in the "golden era."

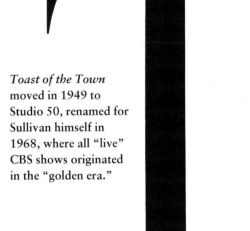

his "biggest" lasted twenty-three years. From 1948 to 1971, every Sunday night at eight o'clock, a man who couldn't sing, or dance, or spin a plate, entertained fifty million Americans. Never before, and never again, would so many gather so loyally, for so long, in the thrall of one man's taste. As if by magic, we were one big family. And what a lot of magic there was, as well as animals and acrobats, ventriloquists and marching bands, David Ben-Gurion, Brigitte Bardot, and the Singing Nun. Not a single act we saw hadn't been handpicked by the awkward impresario, who was a Good Housekeeping Seal of Approval and a Ministry of Popular Culture.

When you think about it, all by himself on CBS Ed Sullivan was a one-man cable television system, with wrestling and Bravo and comedy channels, Broadway and Hollywood and C-SPAN, sports and music video. We turned to him in our living room for everything that we now expect, from an entire industry, twenty-four hours a day: narrative, novelty, and distraction; news and some laughs; snippets of high culture and remedial seriousness and vulgar celebrity; a place to celebrate, and a place to mourn; a circus, and a wishing well, and a cure for loneliness.

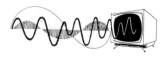

Daily News Broadway columnist Ed, in Hollywood, crowns Tyrone Power and Jeanette MacDonald King and Queen of Filmland in 1939, after a contest sponsored by sixty-two newspapers in the United States and Canada.

There were only three channels to turn to at the start, duking it out for the most desirable hour of the television week. Ed's prime-time competition took the high road (*Philco TV Playhouse* or *Steve Allen*) and the low (*Bowling Stars* and *The Tab Hunter Show*). Jimmy Durante, Perry Como, Eddie Cantor, Bob Hope, and Dean Martin and Jerry Lewis knocked heads against him, and passed out. Among the programs that came and went, while Ed stayed put: *Supper Club; The Big Payoff; The Adventures of Sir Francis Drake; Music on Ice; Bill Dana; Dragnet; Empire; Suspicion; National Velvet; Car 54, Where Are You?; The Original Amateur Hour; Pete Kelly's Blues; Anybody Can Play; Follow the Sun; Grindl; Jamie McPheeters; Arrest and Trial; Hey Landlord; Broadside; Branded; Buckskin;* and *Wagon Train.* James Garner, in *Maverick*, beat him two years running in the ratings, then collapsed from nervous exhaustion.

Back in the days when corporations owned entertainers like household pets, when Arthur Godfrey belonged to Lipton Tea, Jack Benny to Jell-O, Milton Berle to Texaco, Dinah Shore to Chevrolet, and Bob Hope to Pepsodent, Colgate-Palmolive spent $50 million on its *Comedy Hour,* to knock Ed Sullivan out of his Lincoln-Mercury. But he continued once a week to win his time period, until Colgate had to buy a piece of him themselves.

Like Eddie Lopat, the crafty Yankees southpaw, Sullivan seemed to throw nothing but junk, and still they couldn't hit him. How did he do it, this spinning of the public like a plate?

It was a different world. They were making up television as they went along, by the seat of their pants and some sort of bat sonar.

Imagine, at any moment in those prime-time years, a six-room suite on the eleventh floor of the Delmonico Hotel in Manhattan, where Ed Sullivan and his wife, Sylvia, seem to have lived forever. There's a Renoir landscape, his most expensive possession, and a small Gauguin. But there is also a painting by Xavier Cugat, the Cuban bandleader who was the strolling violinist at the Casa Lopez nightclub the night Ed first met Sylvia in 1926. And an original drawing by Walt Disney, in which Ed plays golf with Donald Duck. And autographed pictures of Cardinal Spellman and Ella Fitzgerald. And a framed cover of the October 15, 1955, edition of *Time* magazine that described the television "unstar" this way:

"He moves like a sleepwalker; his smile is that of a man sucking a lemon; his speech is frequently lost in a thicket of syntax; his eyes pop from their sockets or sink so deep in their bags that they seem to be peering up at the camera from the bottom of twin wells. Yet, instead of frightening children, Ed Sullivan charms the whole family."

He gets up at 11 A.M. He breakfasts, invariably, on artificially sweetened pears, iced tea, and a room-service lamb chop. He reads the newspapers and makes hundreds of telephone calls, doing his own dialing. He puts on one of his Dunhill suits — numbered like his shirts and ties so that he can tape a new introduction to an old rerun without looking as though he dropped in on his own program for a surprise visit from Sirius the Dog Star — and a pair of buckled loafers. (His favorite shoes were a gift from George Hamilton, whose feet he once admired.) He takes his lunch, invariably, at Gino's on Lexington Avenue, between 3:30 and 4 P.M., roast chicken, from which he removes and pockets a drumstick, upon which he will nibble later on, wherever he might be in the watches of the night, to the consternation of new acquaintances who are often hungry around him because they never know when to eat; he ticks to a different clock. (His mouth, too, is different: From a childhood bout of scarlet fever and from football injuries in high school, he developed sinus trouble: America's tastemaker can't taste or smell his own food.) He doesn't have a manager, or an agent, or a chauffeur for his limousine, or even a limousine. He likes to talk to the cabbies about his show, as he likes to talk to Lincoln-Mercury dealers. If he is on his way to the studio, he will carry his own change of clothes on a wire hanger in a garment bag. He is without an entourage of sycophants. After the movie screening or the Broadway play, Ed and Sylvia will supper at The Colony or Le Pavillon. He orders sweet wine, which he improves with packets of Sweet'n Low he hoards for that purpose. They are off then to the Yonkers harness races and the frantic nightlife of the clubs.

Ed (right) revising the master plan before a show in 1952: Cut the comic, add a song, lose the chimp . . .

In the early days, with a weekly budget of $375, Ed could only afford to borrow six June Taylor Dancers from Jackie Gleason. Renamed the Toastettes, they pose backstage with Ed (far right) in 1950.

Almost from their first date — a heavyweight prizefight — Ed and Sylvia were self-sufficient, a mollusk of a marriage. They never ate in. Nobody cooked. The only domestic help they needed was the hotel maid. Isn't this odd? Not just the single chop for breakfast, the drumstick in the Dunhill pocket, and the Sweet'n Low for wine, but the peculiar weightlessness, as if the Delmonico were an aquarium: artificial sweetening and artificial light. As in a Hollywood movie or TV adventure series or an experimental novel, nobody ever had to wash a dish or make a bed.

There wasn't much time for reading. In all the literature of Ed Sullivania, the only books mentioned are a biography of Tito, Hedy Lamarr's *Ecstasy and Me*, and *Ivanhoe*. From childhood on, Sir Walter Scott had always been his favorite writer. It's no surprise that in his newspaper column and on his television program, he was romantic, sentimental, and chivalrous. Like Scott, he preferred his damsels in pretty distress, not loudmouthed like Joan Crawford, or overly opinionated like Marlene Dietrich (whom he once called "one of Hitler's cuties") — though we *are* told by a biographer that

Toast of the Town was a hit from its debut on June 20, 1948. Opposite: Peggy Lee sings six weeks later. The Brain Trust (above) decides in 1957 what to do next. Second from left (on Ed's right) is Marlo Lewis, the adman and charities organizer who "discovered" Ed at the Harvest Moon Ball in 1947, pitched the show to CBS, and was his coproducer for the first twelve years.

Ed with comedian Phil Foster and pipe-smoking bandleader-composer Ray Bloch, who would lead the orchestra for the show's twenty-three year run.

"he had to be practically handcuffed when Juliet Prowse was around."

The Sullivans hadn't always lived on the eleventh floor of the Delmonico. Before that, they lived on the twenty-second floor. And before *that*, they lived at the Astor Hotel. There were also a couple of prewar years around a swimming pool in Hollywood where Ed wrote for and acted in several movies so bad you can't rent them. But their days and nights always had this . . . *floating* quality, like the dream life of athletes and gangsters, of actors and comics, show girls and sports, hustlers and swells; songwriters and gag writers and ragtime piano players; men who gambled and women who smoked; Guys and Dolls. Understand that, before television, this was America's dream life,

too, fabricated and syndicated by Broadway columnists like Damon Runyon and Walter Winchell and Louis Sobol and Ed Sullivan — men who had gone to newspapers instead of college.

Newspapers and Broadway: Together, as Ed came of age, they were inventing twentieth century American popular culture. Though vaudeville had been around since the 1880s, its heyday began on Broadway with the Olympia Theatre in 1895; the Victoria, Loew's American, and the Palace in 1913; and the Ziegfeld Follies in 1915. Cheek by jowl the Shubert organization was monopolizing legitimate theater. Shubert Alley was just a couple of blocks from Tin Pan Alley, in the Brill Building on Broadway and 49th, where formulaic popular music was written — first for sheet-music sales; then for musical comedy, records, and radio; finally, for Hollywood and television. Around the vaudeville houses and theaters grew up every variety of dinner-and-dancing restaurant, cafe, and "lobster palace," cabaret and nightclub and Sardi's. In this same Broadway entertainment zone with its billboards and neon, the new radio networks located themselves, and the movie studios established New York offices, and television, with its cumbersome machinery, fought for space. Mass communications, by trial and error, formed a mass taste.

Bootleggers might come and go during the speakeasy years of Prohibition, but the nightlife never stopped. To the north, Madison Square Garden and the 52nd Street jazz clubs. To the south, the Metropolitan Opera and the Seventh Avenue garment district. In between, wigmakers, costume-cutters, set designers, booking agents, and burlesque. (And, just a cab ride away for the after-hours thrillseeker, Harlem.) Whatever else went on behind the shades of rural and small-town, Protestant and middle-class, sober and sexless, heartland America, Broadway was the Big Time and the Big Event, where they dreamed for us all those big-city dreams of license and stardom, where classes and sexes slummed without social distinction in a sea of scandal and celebrity — a democracy of the undaunted and the demimonde; a floating operetta; a rilly big shew.

Or so we were told by the newspaper columnists. Because the newspapers moved to Broadway, too, and magazines like *Vanity Fair* and *The Smart Set* and *The New Yorker.* Broadway, a Coney Island of the mind, was invented by *Variety,* the show-biz daily, and by the Runyons and Winchells who covered the theater, the nightclubs, and every other form of popular entertainment, the way they covered sports. The columnists had all been sportswriters, anyway, before they went to Broadway, and they reported the neon night as if it were one big game, in a permanent present tense, with its own peculiar slanguage of ball-park lingo, stage idiom, underworld argot, immigrant English, fan-speak, black-talk, promoter hype, and pastrami sandwich.

And that's about all they reported, too. They certainly didn't report the political corruption or the racism that have always been the biggest stories in the big city, nor even the real-estate swindles that attended the building of the IRT subway system that brought the crowds to Times Square to begin with. What they wrote, in a wonderful pastiche of Broadway Babel, were press releases for a saloon society of singers like Caruso and fighters like Dempsey and mobsters like Lansky; a fictitious Roaring Twenties where the long legs of the chorus girls went on forever and the gangsters were cute.

In 1953, Ed discovers that he's as much of a celebrity as the stars on his show.

It's important to remember that this was all a dream. Damon Runyon's father, in the wild American West, reported the truth about that glory-hound, Custer. Damon Runyon's father's son didn't report the truth about Pershing in Mexico or Patton in Europe; his famous and shameless rules for the journalism of *his* time were: Never bite the hand that feeds you. And, you go along to get along. Pistol-packing Winchell likewise seldom stirred from his table at the Stork Club, except to tool about town in a cop car listening to the radio; he got enough of what he needed, for the columns that let him bed down with show girls or ruin the careers of homosexuals, leaked on him by eager publicists, or confided to him by that matched pair of his sinister buddies, J. Edgar Hoover and Lucky Luciano. And when he had to go to Hollywood, Winchell could count on Darryl Zanuck to have read-ied for him a private house, on the studio grounds of Twentieth Century-Fox, with servants, sup-plies, and a chauffeur-driven limousine. If any of these "journalists" needed extra cash, they could always emcee a variety show or a radio program, browbeating the talent to attend with the power of their column. Even those Round Table wits at the nearby Algonquin played patty-cake with the pro-ducers, the publicists, and columnists. They were as stagestruck as everybody else on Broadway, and wrote plays about each other, and wound up in Hollywood at the Garden of Allah, drying out or deliquescent, in the throes of a screenplay.

This was Ed Sullivan's gaudy world — from 1922, when he went to work for the New York *Evening Mail,* to 1947, when he was discovered as a *Daily News* columnist who just happened to be emceeing the annual Harvest Moon Ball while CBS just happened to be trying out its primitive cam-eras. Serendipity! Like show biz and sports, like organized labor and organized crime, like the

 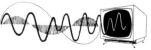

Ed's was the first television show to introduce celebrities from the audience, giving it a one-big-happy-electronic-family feeling. Left: Helen Hayes (1958) and Jimmy Durante (1961).

Mitzi Gaynor (1954).

Janet Leigh (1955).

Jack Dempsey (1961) and Shelley Winters (1955).

Opposite, top: Ed talks to the audience (1964), and jockey Braulio Baeza (1963). Center: toughguy Hawaiian cop Jack Lord (1969) and funnyman Jackie Gleason (1953). Bottom: blue-eyes-to-die-for Paul Newman and friends Glenda Jackson and Richard Chamberlain (1971).

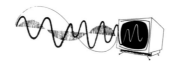

 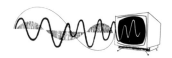

The "unstar" signs autographs in 1955. After decades of covering the sports world and the Broadway theater district as a newspaper columnist, Ed, as a television personality, can no longer walk the streets of New York — or anywhere in the U.S. — unrecognized.

Army and the Church, tabloid journalism had been an agency of upward mobility. But television would prove to be a trampoline . . . a flying carpet.

> *I think everything was wonderful and, look, here I go. It was a simpler era and we all knew who Ed Sullivan was and we knew who we were and we knew what the country was and it was a wonderful time to be a part of it.*
> — JOAN RIVERS

Ed was born September 28, 1902, on East 114th Street, in a part of Harlem that had been mostly Irish, Jewish, and middle class but was changing fast when the Sullivans abandoned it five years later for Port Chester, New York, a small town on Long Island Sound, near the Connecticut border. His twin brother, Danny, died at age nine months, and Ed always felt that if Danny had been around, nobody would have beat up on him. In this era of vulgar psychologizing, we're entitled to wonder if Danny was the one who was supposed to sing songs, tell jokes, tap that dance, spin that plate, tease those cats. Maybe Ed spent the next seventy-two years looking for him. This would also explain why, every Sunday night after his show was over, he always went to Danny's Hideaway. With a nod to Viennese voodoo, we pass on.

His paternal grandfather had come from County Cork in one of those best-selling nineteenth-century potato famines. Ed's father, Peter, was a tough and moody man. The oldest son in a family of eight, he'd gone to work instead of finishing high school, in spite of skills in math and debate; he seems to have resented his patronage job at the New York Customs House. Ed's mother, Elizabeth, was an amateur painter, and a green thumb in the garden, when they finally got one. On the top floor of the two-family Port Chester frame house, in a parlor with velveteen-upholstered furniture, an aspidistra, and an upright piano, there was always music. Peter was partial to opera, especially Melba and Caruso; Elizabeth loved Victor Herbert and John McCormack.

And certainly Port Chester was the sort of town in which an impresario of the democracies of performing talent should have grown up, a ragtime mix of Irish, Italians, Germans, Poles, and Jews, with a factory and a railway station but also a village blacksmith and watering troughs for the horses

Ed and super-assistant Julia Meade play in 1958 with Bil Baird puppets sculpted to look like them. Meade was on the show so often — helping out in comedy skits and advertising spots —Ed took to introducing her as his "cousin."

bought from gypsies to draw the carriages that went to the medicine shows with the snake-oil salesmen. The young Sullivans fresh out of St. Mary's Parochial School could stand by on Boston Post Road and watch the Pierce Arrows, the Packards, and the Model T's chug their way to football games at Yale. Ed pumped the organ at Our Lady of Mercy, for a nickel each Mass. He caddied, with a young Gene Sarazen, for Nicholas Murray Butler, the insufferable president of Columbia University, at the Apawamis Club in Rye. He would also letter in four varsity sports in high school, and run away to Chicago at age fifteen. In Chicago the Marines wouldn't have him, so he returned to his high school newspaper and wrote about sports instead.

Waiting, either for Ed's introduction or for Lawrence of Arabia: camels on 53rd Street, at the side entrance to CBS's Studio 50 in 1957. Sundays before the show, there was usually one or another animal — or a whole drill team or rocker's entourage — on standby in the alley in case a scheduled act ran short or a comedian was canceled.

In celebration of Abraham Lincoln's birthday in 1962, Carl Sandburg, one of the few poets to appear on Ed's show, gives a special tribute.

Opposite: Ed seems to have no idea, in 1961, what unpredictable and off-the-wall Spanish surrealist painter Salvador Dali will do next, and neither does Dali.

Although an uncle offered to pay his way to college, the Port Chester *Daily Item* would pay him to go to games. Who wants more school when you can talk to Babe Ruth? From the ball park, he graduated to the police court and the undertaker's, the manly quick and the manly dead. From Port Chester, after a one-week detour in Hartford, he graduated in 1922 to New York, where the *Evening Mail* hired him to cover college sports. First he had to teach himself to type, with two fingers, by hunting and pecking fair copies of *New York Times* editorials, the closest he ever got to being pompous. Ed's first *Mail* byline was a dog-show story, and his first big interview was with Dempsey, and his first famous buddy was featherweight Johnny Dundee. On the $75 a week they paid him, he lived over Duffy's Tavern, dated flappers, and bought himself a Durant to drive to Flushing each dawn for a round of golf after Ruby Keeler and Jimmy Durante closed the Silver Slipper. The *Mail* sent him to Florida for the winter sports in 1924, then promptly folded. He'd spend the next three years as an AP stringer, a hotel PR man, and bouncing, from the *Ledger* in Philadelphia, to the *World* and the *Bulletin* in New York, to the *Leader*, a socialist newspaper, to the *Morning Telegraph*, a racing newspaper. Talk about your education.

The *Graphic* hired him in 1927. The *Graphic*! Run haphazardly by a health-nut publisher, Bernarr Macfadden, who walked twenty miles barefoot from home to office every morning, the *Graphic* was where Winchell is said to have invented the gossip column, as if there haven't been gossip columns at least since Aristophanes stuck all those fifth century B.C. Athenian poets into his *Batrachoi* and made them croak *Brekekekex ko-ax ko-ax*. Though sports editor Ed still cared more about fun and games than play acting, oh how he envied Winchell the syndication of his column to so many newspapers, and the radio show across the nation, not just for the money, but as much for the dream-like floating life, the hobnobbing insiderness. For four years they feuded, till Winchell was lured away by Hearst's *Daily Mirror*, and Louis Sobol left, too, for Hearst's *Journal American*. Ed was suddenly out of the locker room onto the Great White Way, as a writer instead of a sport. In his first column, on June 1, 1931, he attacked all the other gossip columnists for dishing dirt. But dishing dirt was the why and wherefore of a column and, almost immediately, Ed himself was Winchellizing.

Ed, wife, Sylvia, and daughter, Betty, aboard the Queen Elizabeth in 1950, bound for Europe. Every year Ed and Sylvia went around the world in search of talent for the next season; the show was also broadcast on location from other countries such as Japan, Portugal, France, and Italy.

By June 25, 1931, he led with: "Grover Cleveland Alexander is back with his wife and off the booze." By July 17: "Everyone who played a lead in *The Marriage Circle*, including Lubitsch, the director, has been divorced." By August 13: "Jean Malin belted a heckler last night at one of the local clubs . . . . All that twitters isn't pansy . . . ." The *Graphic* folded a year later, in 1932. A week before it did so Ed was hired by the *Daily News*, where his "Little Old New York" column would appear for the rest of his life.

Everybody who is always saying that Ed's television show was patterned on his newspaper column — the quick pace, with an item for everybody — should understand just how different they were. Of the three cardinal rules for the TV show — open big, keep it clean, and stick in something the kids will like — only "opening big" applied to the newspaper column. Lead with your scoop, whether it's Grover Cleveland Alexander or the Beatles. But there was to be no sex on television — not even any cleavage. Nor would there ever be any unkind remarks about the people we were soon to meet. On TV, everybody was always wonderful. Even the chimps were wonderful.

And so was Fidel Castro. No real journalist would have gone so innocently to Cuba in January 1959 and paid Castro $10,000 to tell the American public, between a trained dog act and Alan King, that "we are all Catholics; how could we be Communists?" Nor would an authentic newspaperman, on being told by Cardinal Spellman that he'd been had by the bearded revolutionary, have refused to cut a new $10,000 check when Castro claimed to have lost the old one. But the whole point of Ed's sort of television was to make the world safe for the middle class.

And Ed's whole point in going on television to begin with was to make more money. He had taken a pay cut, from $375 to $200 a week, moving from the *Graphic* to the *Daily News*. He scrambled to compensate, off his beat, working double shifts on short-lived radio interview programs for CBS and NBC, from places like a table at "21," with sponsors like Adam Hats and American Safety Razor, introducing the likes of Jack Benny, George M. Cohan, Jimmy Durante, Irving Berlin, and Flo Ziegfeld; and on stage, at the Paramount and Loew's State Theatres, as a vaudeville emcee, sometimes for as much as $3,000 a week, although there were five hour-long shows a day. At Loew's State, he also emceed something called the Dawn Patrol Revue. A glance at a typical program — with

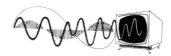

Peg Leg Bates, a one-legged acrobat and tap dancer; and Rita Rio, described by a critic at the time as a singer "in the accepted hot-cha fashion"; and Dave Vine, "one of the most observant of Jewish dialect comics" — tells us all we need to know about where the television program came from, besides Port Chester.

When Ed wasn't on the stage at Loew's State, he was running some benefit or charity drive or dance contest, for the League of Catholic Charities, or the B'nai B'rith, or the Poor Richard Society, or U.S. war bonds. At one such event, the 1947 Harvest Moon Ball, he was discovered, at age forty-five, either by adman Marlo Lewis or by CBS executive Tony Miner, depending on whom you choose to believe. Understand that these men didn't know exactly what they wanted, except *something* the public would look at on this strange new toy, television. Like Mickey Rooney and Judy Garland, they wanted to put on a show in their garage. And here was Sullivan doing it, and he was so ambitious, he'd do it anywhere, and all this mutual neediness ended up making history.

Oh-h, my! Ed Sullivan — in person. That Ed is just the greatest. He's — well, he's like Howard Johnson's. Do you know what I mean? Wherever you are, there'll always be good food and clean rest rooms. —A FEMALE MEMBER OF ED'S STUDIO AUDIENCE

Except with critics and the sponsor, *Toast of the Town* was a hit from its get-go on June 20, 1948. Nobody knew why, and they certainly didn't give Ed credit. Emerson Radio hated Ed, and CBS shopped the show around to anybody who might want it, with or without Ed. Ed would never forgive the network for its lack of confidence. By 1954, his own Sullivan Productions assumed total control of the hour; in 1955 to drive home the point, he changed the name from *Toast of the Town* to *The Ed Sullivan Show.* Years later, in interviews, his scars glowed in the dark.

But that First Sunday, operating on a budget of $375 a week, from a makeshift firetrap of a studio in the tiny Maxine Elliot Theatre — in this Pleistocene era of television, CBS had set up shop near a noisy Grand Central Station; NBC stuck Milton Berle in a converted radio studio; Dumont was located in the damp basement of a Wanamaker's department store — producer Lewis and columnist Sullivan put on a hour that was, probably, the prototype for the next 1,086.

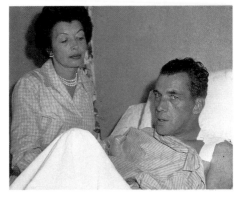

Sylvia visits Ed (left) in the Connecticut hospital where he was recovering from a serious automobile accident in the summer of 1956. He had been driving this car (above) given to him by the show's sponsor, Lincoln-Mercury. The accident, which knocked out his teeth and staved in his ribs, kept him off the air for five weeks.

 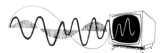

In the hopes of not shocking the audience at home, frightened producers and stagehands tried to subdue anatomical wonder Jayne Mansfield before the Army Show in 1957. Jayne and Ed came up with the idea that she would play the violin.

In another "remote" telecast, this time from Alaska in 1958, Ed poses with Eskimos.

Opposite: Ed and crooner Johnny Mathis in the fast lane on San Francisco's Lombard Street, in, of course, a 1960 Mercury, across the street from a specially equipped CBS mobile unit, from which many "remotes" were shot.

If we don't know for sure, it's because no kinescope has survived. But it certainly *sounds* familiar: Dean Martin and Jerry Lewis, headliners; Richard Rodgers and Oscar Hammerstein, "volunteer" guests; singer Monica Lewis (Marlo's sister), pianist Eugene List, ballerina Kathryn Lee, and "news-maker" John Kokoman, the heroic singing New York City fireman; plus boxing referee Ruby Goldstein, about to handle the Joe Louis-Jersey Joe Walcott championship fight, and six of June Taylor's Dancers, calling themselves "Toastettes." Ray Bloch was there with his orchestra; and Mark Leddy, who would book all Ed's animal acts; and Carmine Santullo, the bootblack from the Bronx who would open Ed's mail and run his copy to the *Daily News* for almost thirty years. It was a tight and loyal crew. Marlo Lewis would be Ed's producer for the next twelve years, till Ed's son-in-law Bob Precht took over.

For the first twenty-six weeks, Ed and Marlo in effect subsidized CBS — using their own phones and office space and secretarial help to keep *Toast* afloat. After thirteen weeks, Emerson Radio bailed out and Lincoln-Mercury took over. Ed was so grateful to the Ford Motor Company that by 1953 he would log more than 250,000 miles as their "ambassador," landing on Boston Common in a helicopter, floating down the Mississippi on a Royal Barge for the Memphis Cotton Carnival. Once, from Paris, he sent picture postcards individually addressed to every Ford dealer. Television was all about selling — a product and a personality. The secret of pacing on Ed's show was that the acts weren't much longer than the commercials. Today on television, half the time, you can't tell the difference. Mark Leddy would tell tell author Jim Bishop: "You wanna know the day Christ died? It was on the Sullivan show and Ed gave him three minutes."

However many minutes Ed gave whomever was decided on that first Sunday, and every subsequent Sunday, by the dress rehearsal that morning in front of a live audience. (After this rehearsal, the audience would be chased out of the studio; a second audience was seated for the real thing in the evening.) Over two decades, much would change in the technical production of the Sullivan hour — it would become the first TV show with a permanent chorus line, and the first to introduce celebrity guests from the audience, and the first to use overhead cameras and rear-screen projections, and the first to go on the road for "remote" telecasts, as well as the first to play with high-resolution cameras, zoom lenses, and videotape, so we saw a Busby Berkeley of singers on water skis,

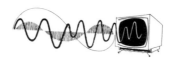

"Now, Dr. King's widow, Mrs. Coretta Scott King, is here with us tonight. All of us sympathize with your terrible grief, and every woman in America envies your courage.**"**

whole choruses of dancers on top of upright pianos, ballerinas twirling in the palm of a baritone's hand, acrobats frozen in midair while a repeat of their triple somersault was "supered in" from another vantage point — but the dreaded rehearsal never changed.

Sunday's rehearsal was Ed's first look at the lineup. As quick as his temper, so, too, was his judgment snappy. If the audience didn't laugh, a comedian was gone, and a singer got an extra song. Add a mime; lose the chimp. Ed trusted his audience even at rehearsals. "Public opinion," he said, "is the voice of God." He was also fond of a dubious assertion by George Arliss that when many people assemble together, "their mass instinct is perilously close to intelligence." What's amazing in retrospect is how seldom God, Ed, and the mass intelligence missed the Royal Barge to Memphis. If Dinah Shore and Nat "King" Cole were booted off the show, because they wanted to plug their new songs instead of singing Ed's hit-parade favorites, well, Pearl Bailey got off her sickbed with a fever of 103 to perform, and Alan King could be counted on to fill any other sudden holes.

Ed does nothing, but he does it better than anyone else on television.   — ALAN KING

It's easy enough to understand why the newspaper critics couldn't stand him. Their hatred of television is notorious and ulterior. But what accounts for his fellow entertainers?

Comedian Fred Allen: "Ed Sullivan will be a success as long as other people have talent."

Comedian Joe E. Lewis: "Ed's the only man who can brighten up a room by leaving it."

Comedian Henny Youngman: "In Africa the cannibals adored him. They thought he was some new kind of frozen food."

Comedian Soupy Sales: "The real reason the circus comes to town is to see Ed Sullivan."

Crybaby Jack Paar: "NBC has its peacock and I think that CBS now has its cuckoo . . . .Who [else] can bring to a simple English sentence such suspense and mystery and drama?"

Carl Reiner was kinder: "Love is like Ed Sullivan. You can't explain its hold on you, but after a while you take it for granted." But when Fred Alien came back to shoot the wounded — "What does Sullivan do? He points at people. Rub meat on actors and dogs will do the same" — Ed was stung to reply, and did so tellingly: "Maybe Fred should rub some meat on a sponsor."

So he looked funny. Even his best friends called him Rock of Ages and the Great Stone Face, the Cardiff Giant and Easter Island, the Miltown Maestro and Toast of the Tomb. He had been, in fact, a handsome man, before an automobile accident in 1956 knocked out his teeth and staved in his ribs. In his early days he was often mistaken for Humphrey Bogart. But after the accident, there was always about him a shadowy wince. He would look more like Richard Nixon — or like Jack

Nicholson in the *Batman* movie playing the Joker *as* Nixon. Oddly, because a media culture is a kind of Silly Putty, what we most remember about Sullivan *and* Nixon are the rubber-faced impressions done of them by impersonators like Will Jordan and David Frye, Larry Storch and Frank Gorshin. Ed and Dick never rolled up their eyes like olives on a slot machine, yet they're fixed that way in our mind's eye: Hogarth snapshots.

A lifelong ulcer didn't help, despite which Ed drank and smoked. (Like Runyon, and like his old enemy Walter Winchell, he would die of cancer.) Nor was he helped by the belladonna he took in his tiny dressing room before he went onstage. (While it expanded the duodenal canal, it also dilated the eyes; Marlo Lewis remembers Ed's having to pump his own stomach just before he went on the air.) Later on, a hearing problem and arteriosclerosis accounted for some of the forgetfulness, those famous malapropisms:

Introducing, in the audience, singer Dolores Gray: "Now starving in a new show . . ."

Forgetting Sergio Franchi's name: "Let's hear it for 'Ave Maria'!"

Mixing up his Antipodes: "the fierce Maori tribe from New England . . ."

Right here in our audience: "the late Irving Berlin!"

When he was really thinking about tuberculosis: "Good night, and help stamp out TV!"

Who knows *what* he was really thinking about? "I'd like to *prevent* Robert Merrill."

He was, perhaps, thinking too much: "Let's hear it reeelly big fer singer José Feliciano! He's blind — and he's Puerto Rican!"

Once, he asked Ray Bloch to strike up the band for guitarist Andrés Segovia, whose act, of course, was a solo. On another occasion, he introduced the Michigan State football team as the University of Michigan football team. They let this stand — but later sent him a birthday cake with his name misspelled.

Coretta Scott King, widow of the assassinated civil-rights leader and Nobel Peace Prizewinner Dr. Martin Luther King, Jr., appears on Ed's stage in 1970 to show film excerpts from her late husband's "Let Freedom Ring" and "I've Been to the Mountain Top" speeches.

 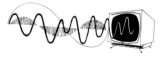

Yet the public loved him, and the stars showed up, and his critics couldn't really attribute the success of the show to his newspaper column. Maybe, in the first few years, Sullivan could and did bully people into appearing on his TV show, as Winchell, Louella Parsons, and Elsa Maxwell had bullied people onto their radio programs with the promise or the threat of their syndicated clout. But it quickly became obvious that Ed's TV show, instead of some sort of tithe entertainers had to pay to get a favorable mention in the *Daily News*, was a career maker; that television was more important than newspapers; that ratings were bigger than readers. When Hedda Hopper tried to compete with him on the cheap, Ed would drive her off the air by insisting, with the help of the unions, that she ante up as much money for her acts as he did, or at least as much as they could get in the nightclubs. Hopper couldn't. Charlton Heston was the first to leave her, and the rest of her press-ganged acts soon followed him, as if from the plagues of Egypt.

And yet Sullivan's success isn't really so very complicated. In his era, he was the best producer in the business. Television is a producer's medium, as movies used to be a director's medium. When we tune in the nightly news on ABC, we may be looking at anchorman Peter Jennings, but what we see is what the executive producer Roone Arledge wants us to see. It's Roone's show. Ed, however, produced and anchored himself; it was as if he had personally invented the Sunday night news. And he got such a transparent kick out of it. Imagine an Arledge coming on: Live, from the Al-Rasheed in downtown Baghdad, Luke Skywalker and the Tracers. Moving right along to palmy Dhahran — the "Wild Weasels" of the Thirty-fifth Tactical Fighter Wing and Raytheon's own antimissile Patriot. From the Pentagon's columbarium, a Rilly Big Shew of "smart" bombs and Pac-Man-Nintendo briefings. Right here on our stage, in weird green cyberspace, a seamless web of Scud alerts, think-tank spindoctors, whey-faced anchorpeople, and Hertz rent-a-generals . . . all bounced off starfish satellites in their network glitterdomes, speaking gee-whiz technoblab . . . The Flying Wallendas play Nuclear Chicken!

Although a man of almost ferocious dignity, Ed permitted himself to pose wearing a rocker fright wig for a July 1965 cover of *Esquire* magazine (far left) and again, in 1970 (left), in front of a painting of the Beatles, because rock and roll had been as good to Ed as Ed had been to rock and roll.

Ed with his son-in-law, Bob Precht, who took over from Marlo Lewis as producer of the show from 1960 till 1971. With Precht's encouragement, Ed introduced to his audiences not only the Beatles but some of the best rock groups in America and England as well as a new generation of comedians.

Which was Ed's other talent. He was so pleased to be exactly where he was, as we ourselves would have been. If he had to leave town, he brought back something he knew we'd like because *he* liked it: a bicycle, a puppet, or a Blarney stone. From Scandinavia, Sonja Henie. From Israel, Itzhak Perlman. From Mexico, Cantinflas. From France, Edith Piaf. From Italy, Gina Lollobrigida. From Russia, the Moiseyev Dance Troupe and, of course, Rudolf Nureyev, paired up with Margot Fonteyn. Like Woody Allen's Zelig, he made every important scene and didn't put on airs about it. In 1955 he confided to readers of *Coronet* magazine which Great Moments in History he wished he could have seen, and you know that if he'd been there, he would have signed them up, just like Dr. Albert Schweitzer: Solomon, making a decision; Socrates, asking questions; the barons at Runnymede, autographing the Magna Carta; the Pilgrims, on Plymouth Rock; Washington, at Yorktown; Lincoln, at Gettysburg; the Wright Brothers, at Kitty Hawk.

> *Appreciation is one of the rarest, most wondrous of God's gifts when it's real, and Ed's is. He is so aware of talent, so struck with the splendors of it — so altogether stagestruck in the true sense of the phrase — that one can actually* feel *it.* — HELEN HAYES

> *Modern man has been fashioned on the basis of exemplary stereotypes: saint, chevalier, caballero, gentleman, Bolshevik, and so on.* — ANDRÉ MALRAUX

Malraux omitted "democrat." Nor would he have even understood the meaning of a word like "fan." But Ed, crucially, was both. From Harlem, and Port Chester, and Broadway, from the ball park and the saloon and the tabloid, all he ever cared about was talent, no matter what it looked like, where it came from, or how he mispronounced it. Forget about the feuds with Arthur Godfrey, Frank Sinatra, Steve Allen, Jack Paar, even Winchell. What we saw on the TV screen was all encompassing. Ed's was the odd sanction of a democratic culture: Anybody could be on his show, but they got there only by being better at whatever they did than everybody else, after which they were certified in their uniqueness, confirmed in their celebrityhood, validated and legitimized. For so long as the culture as a whole knew what it wanted, for so long as it was coherent, then Ed was its "exemplary stereotype."

During the cold war, he was absolutely typical. When the blacklist hit the entertainment industry, he was as craven as the times and as his own network. (At CBS, the Ed Murrows were few and far between. The network fired Joseph Papp as a stage manager because he refused to talk about his friends to a Congressional committee.) In 1950 Hearst columnist Cholly Knickerbocker attacked the Sullivan show for booking dancer Paul Draper and harmonica player Larry Adler, both of whom had been accused of unspecified "pro-Communist sympathies." After Draper appeared on the show, Ed, through his sponsor's advertising agency, apologized to the public: "You know how bitterly opposed I am to communism, and all it stands for . . . . If anybody has taken offense, it is the last thing I wanted or anticipated and I am sorry." Draper and Adler had to leave the country to find work. Likewise, when conductor Arthur Lief refused to tell the House Committee on Un-American Activities whether he'd ever been a member of the Communist party, Ed dismissed him from the orchestra pit for a performance of, ironically, the Moiseyev Dance Troupe fresh from Moscow. Sean O'Casey was dumped from a 1960 St. Patrick's Day tribute for left-wing anticlericalism. Bob Dylan in 1963 was forbidden to sing "The Talkin' John Birch Society Blues." Throughout the disgraceful blacklist period, Sullivan submitted names of performers, for vetting, to the crackpot Theodore Kirkpatrick, the editor of *Counterattack* and author of *Red Channels: The Report of Communist Influence in Radio and Television*, a report that slandered half the entertainment industry.

But then there was the other American obsession: race. At Harry Belafonte, Ed drew a line against the blacklist. From his earliest newspaper days Ed had been a brother. In a column, he'd once attacked New York University for signing a basketball contract with the University of Georgia that required NYU's one black player to stay on the bench. He also set up tournaments for black ballplayers. When his friend Bill "Bojangles" Robinson died, he paid for the funeral at the Abyssinian Baptist Church, anonymously, and organized the parade afterwards to the Evergreen Cemetery in Brooklyn, with an all-star cast of foot soldiers including Berle, Merman, Durante, Danny Kaye, Jackie Robinson, Sugar Ray, and W. C. Handy. When Winchell savaged Josephine Baker, who had been refused service at his favorite Stork Club watering hole, Ed declared a war on the *Mirror* columnist that wouldn't end till one memorable night in 1952 at that same Stork Club, when Ed hustled Winchell into the men's room, pushed his head into a urinal, and flushed him, as if to signify and celebrate the triumph of television over Hearst. And, obliging though he had always been to his sponsor, Ed was contemptuous of those Ford dealers who objected to his on-camera hugging of Ella Fitzgerald, his kissing of Pearl Bailey and Diana Ross. With Louis Armstrong, he'd go anywhere in the world: Guantánamo, Spoleto, Berlin. He loved Motown, and integrated his chorus line so that Bobby Bell, the all-American football player, would have someone his own color with whom to dance, and then wrote an article about it for *Ebony*. From Ethel Waters to Duke Ellington, there wasn't an important black artist who didn't appear on the Sullivan show, just like famous white folks. Black people could star on Ed's TV show long before they could appear in TV commercials. The old sportswriter only cared how they played the game. He had, observed a critic, "an inordinate admiration for champions."

Yes, indeed. A fan and a democrat, with his drumstick and his Sweet'n Low: "Ed Sullivan *lives* democracy," said Ralph Bunche, and it's not a bad epitaph.

Every June, Ed threw himself a TV anniversary party, built around highlights from previous shows. The biggest of these parties was the tenth (right). He aspired to twenty-five years on the air, but missed that mark by two when ratings and network market researchers decided his very long day was done.

Overleaf: On his tenth anniversary, not only Ed but the City of New York pays attention. The motion picture industry unfurls banners in Times Square, and pictures of the former sports reporter and show-biz columnist appear everywhere — even in windows of coffee shops and delis.

But as television expanded — let ninety channels bloom! — the culture fell apart. It was as if the magic, once so concentrated in a handful of choices, had managed somehow to dissipate itself, like an expanding universe after the Big Bang, into chaos or entropic heat-death. By the end of the Sixties, there were twenty variety shows on television, and that wasn't counting the bloody circus in Chicago '68 or the porn movies from Vietnam. Instead of Irving Berlin, Joan Baez. Instead of Broadway, Watts. For more than two decades, Ed Sullivan had not only kept the faith; he had every week renewed it, telling us what was funny, who was important, and how we were to feel about the world he monitored on our behalf. But that world had Balkanized, even in our own homes, where we went like separate tribes to separate television sets and dreamscapes.

Where's the coherence — much less the consensus — when the people who watch *Married . . . With Children* on Fox, and the people who watch ice hockey on cable, and the people who watch *MacNeil/Lehrer* on PBS aren't even speaking to the people who watch Guns n' Roses on MTV?

There is no more Ed Sullivan show; it's amazing there ever was. Such innocent bonds, such agreeable community, so much Broadway, Tin Pan Alley, and Port Chester. Today, we'd probably describe such a show as "postmodern." Although heavyweight intellectuals have a hard enough time defining "modernism," it has something to do with extreme subjectivity, historical impasse, apocalyptic apprehensions, technological alienation, and a uniquely modern form of salvation — of, by, and for the self; a permanent revolution of style and sensibility. *Post*modernism knows all this, and makes fun of it, which means lots of sensational publicity for anything odd; crazy juxtapositions of the high culture and the low; random, meaningless lists; cartoons, parodies, and fragments. Postmodernism (or postindustrial, or postfeminist, or poststructuralist, or Post Toasties) is kind of Campy: nostalgia laced with contempt. And that's what Ed looks like at the Museum of Television and Radio. But back then, *he didn't know it and neither did we*. Ed was *before* we'd all become so guileful in our self-consciousness that we got it down to a disease; before we decided that television itself is one big postmodern Pandora's box.

Another
maisel
RESTAURANT

INTRODUCING
the ultimate in
DELICATESSEN

Special
Maisel's

Hamburger
Served with
PICKLES · RELISH

39¢

Maisel's
SALUTES
Ed Sullivan ON HIS
10TH ANNIVERSARY
ON WCBS-TV

BE SURE TO SWITCH TO
CHANNEL **2**
SUNDAY NIGHT AT 8

COMEDY

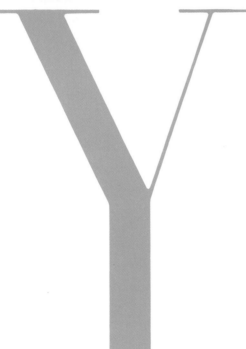

Comedian Will Jordan, in 1954, was the first to impersonate Ed on his own show. A friend had told Ed that Jordan did a better imitation of him than Ed himself. Ed went to see him, thought so too, and booked him thirteen times. Many others — including John Byner, David Frye, and Jackie Mason — would later impersonate Ed.

You had to go to the Delmonico and make him laugh. At home with his room-service lamb chop, he insisted on hearing every word. From singers and dancers and acrobats and magicians, from trained bears and Italian puppets, all that he required was passing muster at the Sunday dress rehearsal. But comedians never got to that rehearsal until they'd gone, on a Wednesday or Thursday, to Ed's hotel, up the elevator and into the Temple of Karnak: Amuse me. Just imagine the court jesters. André Malraux in *Antimemoires* reports having gone once to the Soviet Union, where he spent a weekend at Gorky's dacha with Stalin and Molotov. They talked about Laurel and Hardy. Thinking he had dropped his passport, Malraux looked under the table, "and what do I see? . . . Stalin, Molotov, and the rest of them trying to twist their fingers like Stan Laurel." It must have been like that — except that Stan Laurel would have had to have been there himself, with his fingers crossed as well as twisted.

The so-called "Nairobi Trio" in 1958; inside one of these monkey suits, Ernie Kovacs himself, a kind of Hungarian Robin Williams.

Comedy mattered more to Ed than any other act. It wasn't just that he loved to laugh, but he also knew instinctively that comedians are dangerous; that's the thrill of them. It's a high wire of language, without any net: Surprise us, but not unpleasantly. Ed could have any comedian he wanted, from Will Jordan to Mort Sahl, stand-up or skit, Wayne and Shuster doing their riffs on Shakespeare, Phil Silvers with a banana. They didn't have to adapt to any House Style of humor; they wouldn't be competing with their host, who wasn't a Milton Berle or Jackie Gleason.

But Ed was there to entertain the Republic, not subvert it. He belonged to, indeed exemplified, an era when comedy was supposed to make us feel *better* about ourselves instead of worse. He'd been mystified at first by Richard Pryor, who made the cut at the Delmonico but was dropped once after rehearsal. He was more comfortable with Flip Wilson and Moms Mabley, or the impressionist George Kirby, even Nipsey Russell. Black people who sang, danced, or boxed were more readily translatable into terms a mainstream, middlebrow culture could appreciate than were blacks who rubbed us like a rasp. And he was most comfortable with the Catskills comics like Myron Cohen, Sam Levenson, Henny Youngman, and Jack E. Leonard. He was so comfortable with Alan King that King could skip the Delmonico auditions.

Though Marilyn Monroe was one of the few superstars who never appeared on *The Ed Sullivan Show*, comedienne-singer Edie Adams, Ernie's wife, does a hot imitation.

Opposite: As always in a Jackie Gleason routine, the timing was critical and the world was unkind. Here, in 1952, an Automat bites back.

COMEDY

A rogues' gallery of the classic comedians who worked the Sullivan stage: Storied Catskills vaudevillians Myron Cohen (top) and Jack Carter (center left), who made forty-three and forty-nine appearances respectively; Mr. Television himself, Milton Berle (center right), on one of his rare guest shots on a competing show; Ed's old friend Phil Silvers (bottom left), who also lived in the Delmonico Hotel; a just-starting-out Bob Newhart (bottom right), who would move on to star in his own TV series.

Also making us laugh: Regulars Marty Allen and Steve Rossi (below left); George Carlin (below right), before he got into so much trouble with the Federal Communications Commission for using the forbidden words it never would have occurred to him to utter on Ed's program; and Richard Pryor (bottom), whose thirteen appearances would help change the direction of American humor.

Back in the dewy dawn of the New Neuroticism, Woody Allen was King. With nothing standing between him and his audience, Woody talks, of course, about his childhood.

Flip Wilson (left) in 1967, another of Ed's favorites who got his own show, and Totie Fields (below left), from vaudeville nights and vaudeville days, in 1964, her fifth appearance out of a total of twenty.

Opposite: One of Ed's favorite comediennes, Phyllis Diller, in 1960, in one of her classic poses. She claims to have created this persona first, with its fright wig, gloves, and cigarette in a holder, and then put her comedy to work around it.

Frank Gorshin (above right), who also impersonated Ed, doing Kirk Douglas in 1961, and Imogene Coca (formerly of Sid Caesar's *Your Show of Shows*) looking Rhine Maiden-Wagnerian in 1957 (right).

Alan King in 1957, on his second of thirty-seven appearances. King, one of Ed's golf buddies almost always on call from Great Neck to fill a five- or ten-minute hole in the show, was so reliable he didn't have to rehearse his routine, and would not be stuck anywhere near a rock group, whose screaming teens threw off his timing and missed the point of his New York punch lines.

He was partial as well to impressionists, from Jordan, who invented the Sullivan parody, to John Byner, George Carlin, Johnny Carson, Jack Carter, Sammy Davis, Jr., Arnold Dover, Frank Gorshin, Rich Little, and Jackie Mason, who all imitated Jordan imitating Ed. Humor on television was turning into humor *about* television, at least on Ed's show. Next door, Sid Caesar, Imogene Coca, and Carl Reiner still made fun of movies and opera.

Still, Pryor was on thirteen times, one more than Flip Wilson, twelve more than Bill Cosby, and about as often as Lucille Ball and Rowan and Martin, Joe E. Lewis and Jan Murray. Getting a little more air time were Allen and Rossi, Bill Dana, Shelley Berman, Victor Borge, Totie Fields, Bert Lahr, Joan Rivers, Smith and Dale, and Nancy Walker. Then there were the elite: Stiller and Meara (thirty-six times), Cohen (forty-three) and King (thirty-seven), and Canadians Wayne and Shuster (an astonishing fifty-eight appearances). A man who lives most of his life in the same hotel likes to be comfortable, doesn't like surprises, and tends to play favorites.

Besides, the show itself, live television, tended enough toward nervous breakdown, without the unpleasant surprise of comics' freaking out. Even after the Delmonico audition and those Sunday rehearsals where a Sid Caesar and Nancy Walker skit was abruptly canceled and Woody Allen earned himself a Big Ed tongue-lashing for having talked dirty, things went wrong. Not only the animals got out of control. There was the infamous evening of October 18, 1964. The featured comic was Jackie Mason, up till then one of Ed's best buddies. You can think of Mason as one of the many casualties of Vietnam. They had been forewarned that LBJ would interrupt the show about halfway through to say something about the war, but they expected him to be brief. He wasn't — and no one knew how long he'd go. By the time the show was back on "live," Jackie was in the middle of his monologue, already annoyed at having been placed last on the program where he'd had to compete with the President. Sullivan began a frantic series of hand signals: *two minutes*. The audience found Ed as amusing as Jackie; they were ignoring his punch lines.

" My philosophy about television is quite simple — all I can do is dig up the very best possible acts, introduce them as courteously as I know how, and then get out of their way. **"**

Godfrey Cambridge appeared only once on the Sullivan show, in 1971, where he presented Ed with an Afro wig, which he described as an "Honorary Negro Award."

Hollywood High graduate Carol Burnett, later to appear on *The Garry Moore Show*, debuted on Sullivan's stage January 6, 1957, the very same night that the whole nation only saw half of Elvis.

As if acquainted with the strange secret powers otherwise possessed only by the ancient Rosicrucians, Soupy Sales was able to talk Ed into appearing as a grandmother in 1965.

Bert Lahr and Nancy Walker (above) in 1961, doing their famous delicatessen sketch, which Walker went on to do later with other partners.

Jerry Stiller and Anne Meara, together in 1969 as always (above), for their thirty-sixth appearance on the Sullivan show. Here he's TV newsman Walter Flonkite interviewing her as Mrs. Mulcahy, whose son is rioting at the school across the street.

Sid Caesar (second of fifteen appearances) and Joyce Jameson (her one and only) in a 1965 "Shadow Waltz" sketch mocking Central European royalty of the *Student Prince* sort.

His name: José Jimenez,
a.k.a. Bill Dana, this
time, in 1963, as an
astronaut.

Dan Rowan and Dick
Martin in 1961, one of
their fifteen times on
Ed's show before
Laugh-In made them —
and Goldie Hawn and
Lily Tomlin — almost
as famous as Sullivan.

Take My Catskills,
Please: George Jessel
(above left), 1961;
Morey Amsterdam
(above right), 1967;
Henny Youngman
(bottom left), 1967; and
Rodney Dangerfield
(bottom right), 1968,
not getting any respect
even in the fifth of
fifteen appearances.

Opposite: Victor Borge
with the best seat in the
house, in 1960, trying
to decide whether he
will make fun of his
piano or our
punctuation.

COMEDY

Carl Reiner interviews
two-thousand-year-old
Mel Brooks in 1961.

Vaughn Meader, in
October 1962, doing
the John F. Kennedy
impersonation that sold
a million albums and
ceased to be funny a
little more than a year
later.

Shelley Berman, the first
telephone comedian, in
one of the earliest (1958)
of his twenty-one
appearances.

Bill Cosby, in 1964,
before *I Spy* and the
Huxtable obstetrics.

Mort Sahl, in 1960, one of the first comedians to bring cutting-edge political humor to the Sullivan show.

David Frye, considered by many to be the best of the impressionists, doing his Lyndon Johnson imitation in the war year of 1966.

So Jackie started making fun of Ed's hand signals. This is when, according to Ed, Jackie gave him and the audience that storied middle finger. Ed's fury cost Mason $37,500 on a canceled five-show contract and after nineteen appearances, Mason was off the show and out of favor. They'd reconcile two years later, after a chance meeting in the Las Vegas airport, but Jackie's career went into a slide that lasted fifteen years in such gulags as the Catskills and your seedier nightclubs. Even today, he'll talk your head off on the subject, still missing the point, which is that even way back then, in 1964, Vietnam was already starting to ruin everybody's fun.

You know that we would have seen more of Dean Martin and Jerry Lewis, Steve Allen, Jack Benny, Milton Berle, George Burns, Red Buttons, Sid Caesar, Johnny Carson, Wally Cox, Jimmy Durante, Jackie Gleason (and Art Carney), George Gobel, Bob Hope, Ernie Kovacs, Bob Newhart, Jack Paar, Carl Reiner, Phil Silvers, Red Skelton, and Dick Van Dyke — if they hadn't gone on to shows of their own often in competition with Ed; or if Mort Sahl hadn't gotten strange about the Kennedy assassination, and Woody Allen hadn't wanted to be Bergman and Fellini. For whatever reason, once was enough for Ed when it came to David Brenner, Charlie Callas, Pat Harrington,

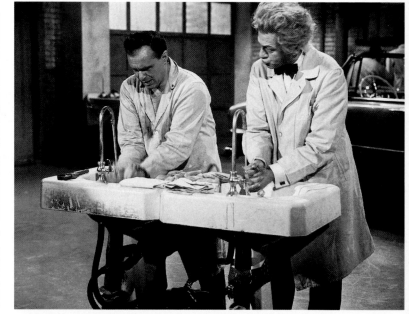

Popular Music

Singers like Peggy Lee remained popular with Ed and his audiences for three decades. Seen here with Sullivan (below) in 1950 and (right) in 1962, singing a medley of "The Sweetest Sounds," "I'll Get By," and "I Believe in You," Lee was able to infuse standard Tin Pan Alley music with her own jazzy flair.

Tin Pan Alley wasn't Abbey Road or Penny Lane or even down to the end of Lonely Street, at Heartbreak Hotel. But before television, even before radio, Tin Pan Alley was where they made up the songs that told us who Americans are supposed to be and how we ought to feel, the way Hollywood would make up movies that were valentines to an apple-pie myth of America. Since the turn of the century, popular music was produced and exploited from a centrally located area in New York City that got the name Tin Pan Alley because of all the noise being made along those streets as songwriters tried to sell their wares to tough-minded music publishers. More often than not, the songs' composers, like the movies' producers, were the children of immigrants for whom the myth was wish fulfillment, as if the melting pot were a machine for spinning cotton candy.

Tin Pan Alley was as much a state of mind as a New York neighborhood. Whatever the public seemed to want, it provided — sentimental ballads, comical immigrant medleys, Broadway show tunes, ragtime, and blues songs like "Hello! Ma Baby" and "Bill Bailey, Won't You Please Come

Welsh heartthrob Tom Jones, who parlayed seven appearances on the Sullivan show, as well as guest shots everywhere else on the dial, into his own TV program, sings a medley of his hit recordings "It's Not Unusual," "Delilah," and "Danny Boy" in 1968.

Home?" (both written by white males). By the time Ed Sullivan was a cub sports reporter, Tin Pan Alley had moved into the Brill Building at 1619 Broadway, where the ASCAP composers who seemed to live there published and sold their sheet music in the millions of copies. The recording companies depended on them. From the radio stations that played this music, ASCAP collected hefty fees. And the music itself was written to be sung by everybody and anybody, for a royalty.

It's not fair to say that all Tin Pan Alley music sounded just the same. If it was all formula, within that formula a Cole Porter and a Harold Arlen got tricky indeed; George and Ira Gershwin bent the forms out of shape; even Irving Berlin was astonishingly dexterous, from "Alexander's Ragtime Band" to all the songs in *Annie Get Your Gun*. But with repetition, the sarcasm and the sting seemed to disappear, the cynicism and the bitterness of those songwriters with more on their minds than feel-good music turned into a security blanket of sound, the sort of soothing soup we're served today in elevators, at piano bars, in the mall, or in Las Vegas. In Ed's day it was the music of the clubs and the radio, and since what he was up to on his show was the bringing of the clubs and radio to the small screen, Tin Pan Alley was for years mostly what we heard, a kind of score for Ed's home movie of America the innocent, the wholesome, and the consensual: Howard Keel instead of Paul Robeson.

When Sergio Franchi, whom Ed discovered in Italy, was able to hit the really big note in "Core'ngrato" on his television debut in 1962, he hit the really big time. Sullivan invited him back on the show twenty-three times thereafter. He is seen here (right) in 1963.

Opposite: Ed liked Pearl Bailey so much she appeared on his show twenty-three times, and once, unexpectedly and unrehearsed, he even danced with her. He was also criticized, by Lincoln-Mercury dealers among others, for giving her a hug. So he made a point of giving her another one. Here, in 1962, she's singing Rodgers and Hammerstein's show tune "Getting to Know You."

Pat Boone, the parents'
answer to Elvis Presley,
is seen here in 1962,
singing "Days of Wine
and Roses." Not seen
here are his white buck
shoes.

Kate Smith, in 1963,
who took America
through World War II
on a wing and a prayer,
brought them through
the Fifties and Sixties on
the Sullivan show
singing everything from
"God Bless America" to
"What Kind of Fool
Am I?"

In her white habit, Sister
Sourire, the Belgian
"Singing Nun," does her
Number One jukebox
hit "Dominique" in
1963 — a scoop for Ed,
in gratitude for which
he, through his Catholic
connections, gave
her convent the jeep
they needed.

Tiny Tim (left), who camped his way through "Tip-Toe Thru' the Tulips With Me," sings, implausibly, "Great Balls of Fire" in 1968. Nancy Sinatra, famous for "These Boots Are Made for Walkin'," sings "Love Eyes" in 1967 (below), after which she'll join Lee Hazlewood for "Summer Wine."

"Look who's assembling on our stage tonight . . ."

A very young Wayne Newton, before he became Mr. Las Vegas, sings "Hello, Dolly" and "Bill Bailey, Won't You Please Come Home?" in 1965.

Opposite: Hopscotching the world for headliners, Ed came back with the Russian Moiseyev Ballet (top left), leaping over the iron curtain, and the Barbados Police Band (top right), helping bring the limbo into America; the Tokyo Happy Coats (center left), one of Japan's first female groups, singing "Bye Bye Birdie" Dixieland-style, and the Sponono Dancers from South Africa (center right), exporting their culture; Mexico's mariachis

(bottom left), fiddling under sombreros, and an Israeli dance troupe (bottom right), souping up the hora.

This page: Ed welcomes a Balinese dancer (top left), is entertained by a Korean church choir (center left), and presents the Royal Welsh Male Choir (bottom), singing "Men of Harlech" in tuxedos. The Rosario Galan Ballet (center right) demonstrates why flamenco is *the* popular music of Spain.

Overleaf: Ed admires Liberace's remarkable coat (left), just before Liberace performs "Impossible Dream." For a 1970 salute to Richard Rodgers at the Hollywood Bowl, Johnny Mathis and Mama Cass Elliot (right), dressed for success, sing "My Favorite Things."

Ann-Margret (left) sings the title song from the movie version of *Bye Bye Birdie,* in which there was not only a part for Ed but a hymn to his name as well. Della Reese (right), in 1957, sings "I Only Want to Love You."

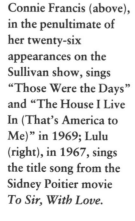

Connie Francis (above), in the penultimate of her twenty-six appearances on the Sullivan show, sings "Those Were the Days" and "The House I Live In (That's America to Me)" in 1969; Lulu (right), in 1967, sings the title song from the Sidney Poitier movie *To Sir, With Love.*

British songbird Petula Clark (above), smaller than the jukebox on which her Top Ten songs were played, sings "I Know a Place" in 1965. She would later sing all her other hits on the show, including "Downtown" and "Don't Sleep in the Subway."

Liza Minnelli and Judy Garland both sang on the Sullivan show, but never together. Here Liza (above) delivers a rock medley and "If I Were in Your Shoes" in 1970. Lesley Gore (below) does her huge hit "It's My Party" in 1963.

Dionne Warwick (top), in 1967, sings "The Way You Look Tonight" and looks, amazingly, the way she does today after so many other Burt Bacharach songs.

Connie Stevens (center) sings "Wild Is the Wind" on a show in which she was honored, along with Paula Prentiss and Troy Donahue, as "Hollywood's Most Popular and Versatile Performers of 1962." Julie Wilson (left) doing a 1962 Cole Porter medley.

Ferrante and Teicher, in 1961, doing their famous and inescapable theme from *Exodus,* the Movie and the Guilt.

Eddie Fisher, somewhere between Debbie Reynolds and Elizabeth Taylor, on one of his ten appearances on the show, sings "The Sweetest Sounds."

My favorite story is the one about the horse. This horse was attached to the buggy that was pulling Frankie Laine across the stage, followed by a bunch of dancers, with Frankie singing "I Believe." Timed perfectly, just when Frankie got to the lyric, "I believe for every drop of rain that falls, a flower grows," the horse decided to relieve its bladder. This gush lasted, according to Marlo Lewis's stopwatch, a full thirty-two seconds, long enough to spray the dancers up to their knees and seize the audience with giggle and guffaw. As Frankie was about to leave his buggy for the church, the horse topped himself with an enormous turd. In the panicked control room, they ordered new and contradictory shots to avoid the sloshing and slopping, but the cameramen kept falling down. Frankie stayed put in the carriage, but he did finish the song, with Ray Bloch and the music in reasonable proximity. They deserved their standing ovation.

But there were other reasons for the audience of *The Ed Sullivan Show* to stand up and cheer. Ed brought on the great voices — an Ethel Merman and a Pearl Bailey — who would sometimes blast through the wax in our ears. What Ella Fitzgerald and Sarah Vaughan did to the standards was as remarkable as what the alchemists used to do to metals, except this time we got gold. Liza Minnelli and her mother knew how to stop a show. Lena Horne, Peggy Lee, Della Reese, Nina Simone, and Dionne Warwick knew how to slow it down and make it think. Likewise, the Big Bands like Tommy Dorsey, Benny Goodman, Woody Herman, Harry James, Gene Krupa, Glenn Miller, and Paul Whiteman altered whatever they touched. Though the show may not have had the hard-edge avant-garde sound of the Charlie Parkers and the John Coltranes, it did give us the Cab Calloways, Count Basies, Duke Ellingtons, Erroll Garners, Dizzy Gillespies, and Lionel Hamptons; the Dave Brubecks and Stan Kentons. And though Al Hirt may have given us a commercialized Bourbon Street version of Dixieland jazz, Sullivan found for us entertainment subcultures from the country of Johnny Cash and the gospel of Mahalia Jackson to the early wonders of world music: a Trini Lopez, a Miriam Makeba, and a Ravi Shankar.

Folk dancers arrived as if by cargo hold and forklift from Warsaw, Prague, and Cuba; from Mexico, Brazil, and Ireland; from Romania, New Guinea, Africa, and Japan. We even got the Soviet

Ed with some of the
most popular
songstresses of the
Fifties. Dinah Shore
(top right) went on to
have a show of her
own; Teresa Brewer
(above) appeared more
than thirty times
because her songs were
always at the top of the
charts; Rosemary
Clooney (right), likewise
a Fifties chart-buster, is
about to sing "This Ole
House" in 1955.

Herb Alpert (above) takes the Tijuana Brass into a "Taste of Honey" in 1965.

Opposite: While Al Hirt brought his New Orleans jazz band onto the show fourteen different times, here he performs "I'm on My Way" in 1963.

Redoubtable folk-gospel mistress Odetta gives a "Shout for Joy" in 1960.

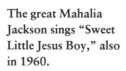

The great Mahalia Jackson sings "Sweet Little Jesus Boy," also in 1960.

In 1969, her last of five performances on Ed's stage, Cyd Charisse dances to "MacArthur Park," where they left a cake out in the rain.

Union's Red Army Dancers. We also got some of the great dance interpreters of Tin Pan Alley music — Fred Astaire and Cyd Charisse, Gene Kelly and Ann Miller, Bojangles and Chita Rivera, Marge and Gower Champion and Juliet Prowse, the Copa Girls and the Cancan. The very existence of the June Taylor Dancers bespoke a commitment to the most athletic of the performing arts, to more breaking of the laws of gravity than we would ever see again till Michael Jordan.

Country would do terrible things to Tin Pan Alley when it discovered how to plug its own songs on radio. Rock on radio — and on television, once producer Precht identified the existence of that distinct "teen" audience Dick Clark was already going after on another channel — would take this elevator music down to hell. The Metalheads and Punks would write graffiti all over the walls of the mall, and sometimes swastikas. Rap and hip-hop would tell us something about our mythical America that Tin Pan Alley had done its best to cover up. We all listen to our own separate musics now on our own color- and class- and sex- and generation-specific stations, through Walkman head-sets, when we aren't tuned in to hate radio. Do we miss Ed, and the consensus? Sure we do — like Captain Kangaroo and Ferdinand the Bull and the Great Pumpkin and all the other friends of our vanished childhood.

Peg Leg Bates, a favorite of Ed's from his Loew's Theatre vaudeville days — fifteen appearances — does a 1962 tap.

Peter Gennaro and his dancers "Alouette" in 1967. Gennaro also choreographed Ed's show, like Bob Fosse and Hugh Lambert, but more often.

Overleaf: Two performers who were able to turn popular songs into great moments in American music: Eartha Kitt sings "I Love Him" and "What Is This Thing Called Love?" in 1956. Bobby Darin rehearses "Mack the Knife" and "Beyond the Sea" in 1962.

Ed, in 1961, put on one of the winning couples (above) from the annual *Daily News*-sponsored Harvest Moon Ball dance contest; Juliet Prowse (right), the dancer who went from South Africa into Elvis Presley movies, performs "My Heart Belongs to Daddy" in 1964.

NOVELTY

Physical comedian Richard Hearne (top), better known as Mr. Pastry, demonstrates to Ed, in 1964, the infamous British chair-jumping test; Ed chats, in 1962, with Nate Eagle & Co. (center) from the Ringling Brothers circus; Big Ed contemplates a Little Ed who talks back (below), courtesy of Bil Baird puppetry in 1951, the second of Baird's thirteen appearances on the show.

From childhood days in Port Chester, with the medicine shows and the three-card monte, Ed loved everything that was cunning and weird in the way people made a living and their art, the way they used their wits. Look at him admiring them, like a wise child.

While there may be far too many tap dancers still around, when was the last time you saw a ventriloquist on prime-time television, or an accordion? The same goes for animals. Like magicians, they sometimes show up on David Letterman, but almost always in a context of ridicule, like his Stupid Pet Tricks. At least on TV, even the circus has lost its savor. We are surrounded by vegetarians and antivivisectionists, and our whole kinky relationship with the animal and vegetable kingdoms has been called into question. When we look into the mad eyes of a Furry Other, we only seem to see our mirrored selves, even if what's really going on inside that alien head is probably the tantrum of some overrated instinct, some helpless heat. We could and should have learned from Ed.

Perhaps more than the Beatles, or Elvis, or Ed's "little friend from Italy," Señor Wences (above) is who we remember after so many years — and so many appearances (twenty-three of them). S'all right? S'all right! Professor Backwards (left) was a successful mixture of Southern humor and vaudeville showmanship.

> **"**For all the youngsters
> in the country, here's
> one of the all-time
> favorites of our show,
> the little Italian
> mouse, Topo Gigio.**"**

Topo Gigio (above),
in one (1963) of
his innumerable
appearances, was so
well known that truck
drivers pulled up beside
Ed's cab and shouted,
"Kees-a-me, Eddie!"

———

Jim Henson's Muppets
(below), seen here in
1971, had been Ed's
guests twenty-five times
before they got a show
of their own called
Sesame Street.

From 1961, one of seven appearances by Zippy the Monkey, who jumped through a hoop on roller skates before dropping them on Ed's foot, and then rode a bicycle into the camera.

Julia Meade, for instance, remembers a night on the show when Ed pulled the lion tamer to one side just a minute before he was supposed to go on camera. "Look," said Ed, "we've got to cut you down to three minutes. Do you understand?" "Yeah," said the lion tamer, "I understand, but how am I going to explain it to the lion?"

Nobody explained it to the lions and tigers when Clyde Beatty, every spiffy inch of him the Great White Hunter in pith helmet and safari suit, discovered too late that he had only forty-eight square feet of cage space to work with on the Sullivan stage, instead of the obligatory minimum of fifty-two. Finding their imperious tormentor within surprisingly easy reach, the cats ripped the shirt off his safari suit. Beatty bolted through his escape hatch. Ed directed the cameras into the audience. While Beatty was trying to wrap it up early, and the stagehands were trying to strike the set, the cats lost their composure and all hell broke loose. According to an eyewitness, "The lions are pounding the shit out of the tigers." What you saw on the screen was Ed's mouth, opening and closing, but you couldn't hear a word for the roar onstage, where a beleaguered Beatty was hitting them with whips and chairs. And there wasn't time to clean the stage before the next act, so the romantic dance team had to slide through the, ah, residue of the cats' excitement.

Richiardi the Magician
loses one of his female
assistants in 1961.

Pompoff and Thedy
hear a different music
in 1966.

Pigmeat Markham and
Chuck Thompson play
with lemons in 1961.

Baby Opal (top right, sitting down) was on thirteen times; Russ Burgess (center), for the birds, disappeared after a single appearance; at the behest of Captain James Tibor, Smaxie and Maxie (bottom right) performed like seals in 1962.

Opposite: Paul Sydell and his wonder dog Suzy in 1962.

Tony the Horse and
Rosaire his Trainer
(above) in 1961. Ed
goes Russian, and
maybe cossack, in one
of four shows that
featured the Moscow
Circus, in 1963 (right).

Carl "the Amazing" Ballantine took his comedy-magic act from Sullivan in 1957 to a regular role on the *McHale's Navy* TV series.

Ed always had trouble with bears. On one memorable occasion, man and bear were supposed to wrestle, center stage, on a mat. The bear for his good behavior was supposed to get a double-scoop ice-cream cone. A stagehand gave Ed the ice-cream cone, and he wandered from his mark to get a better view of the action, and the cone dripped, and Ed absentmindedly licked at it, and the bear did a double take, lunging at the gossip columnist for the daily newspaper with the largest circulation in America. While the trainer's wife rushed onstage with a pistol, the trainer tackled the bear. For at least two weeks thereafter, Ed stayed close to his mark.

Then there were the Russian bears. After riding their bicycles, they went after the audience. Television verité! "Get those goddamned Communist killers out of my theater!" screamed Ed.

But you probably want to hear about Topo Gigio and Señor Wences. I'd rather talk about Señor Wences, a personal enthusiasm, except there's nothing to say. S'all right? S'all right. This little Italian mouse, of whom everybody eventually wearied though not soon enough, was so often featured on the show — maybe it just *seemed* more often than Jack Carter or Wayne and Shuster — to "humanize" Ed. Tired of hearing about his Great Stone Face, he wanted somebody to kiss it. (In this, Topo was a co-conspirator with all the impressionists who did Ed. The boss was insisting: I do, *too*, have a sense of humor.) But when even truck drivers, pulling up beside his cab, cried out, "Kees-a-me goo' night, Eddie," they fed the rodent to one of Beatty's cats. "Frankly," said talent coordinator Jack Babb, "I think we wore the little bastard into the ground."

Jim Henson's Muppets went on to greater glory on *Sesame Street*, which is more than one can say, or would want to, about Alvin and the Chipmunks. If we can't remember the name of the dog that played the piano, Lady was the elephant on water skis. Who will ever forget Papsie Georgian, doing the Hawaiian hula on a paddleboard; or Mayana, so scared that Markworth, on an off night,

Shari Lewis (above)
introduced Lambchop
and friends to a
television audience that
remained faithful for
thirty years. Rickie
Layne and Vel Vel
(below), seen here with
Ed in 1964, were just
one example of Ed's
continuing enthusiasm
for ventriloquists. These
two tried to teach him
how to do it himself.

Pantomime duo Les
Doubles Faces, in 1965,
bouncing about a
disembodied head in
TV's two-dimensional
twilight zone.

Opposite: In 1956,
contortionist Piet Von
Brechts had the
audience in stitches and
himself in knots.

In the first (1967) of three appearances, the Jovers — Fe and Wilfred Halliwell (left) — imagine they're a windmill as they pursue their own impossible dream.

Opposite: The unlikely Unus (top left) perches gingerly on Ed's stage. A blindfolded Markworth shot the arrows, a terrified Mayana wore the balloons (top right), and neither was ever seen again on Ed's show after this appearance in 1966. Helene and Howard discover performance art in 1965 (bottom left). Fresh out of oranges in 1962, Leo Bassi (bottom right) instead juggles a piano.

would put an arrow in her ear that she needed a few stiff shots to stop shaking; or Jill Corey, singing "I'm Sitting on Top of the World" on top of the Mendenhall Glacier in Alaska — though anything you could do at all on live television from Alaska was a novelty act, like poor George Bruno on his sway pole in Kotzebue, high above the Arctic Circle, in a sixty-mile-an-hour breeze, at ten degrees below zero: When he climbed up with his bare hands, the skin on his palms tore off and stuck to the pole like table scraps. Even worse was when the Wallendas tried their seven-man pyramid, on a cable stretched across Eighth Avenue one windy gale-force night, 150 feet up without a net.

Well then, dancing horses, bears on bikes, chimps on motorcycles, pandas on roller skates; fire eaters, sword swallowers, sponge divers, mind readers, ice jugglers, limbo dancers; James Tibor's seals, John Tio's parrot, a dachshund that did arithmetic, and the Kilgore College Rangerettes; Old Bill the Navy Goat and Mr. Pastry the English comic and Wernher von Braun the Nazi rocketeer; the Doodletown Pipers, Kuban Kossacks, Australian jugglers, Swiss yodelers, Polish glockenspielers, Jayne Mansfield's violin and Jayne Mansfield's breasts . . . almost as surprising as the fact that animals and people could do these things was the fact that animals and people should want to.

Upon mature reflection, it seems to me we need an expanded definition of what constitutes "novelty" when we speak of the Sullivan show. What about Leo Durocher *and* Buddy Holly? Danny Kaye *and* Duke Kahanamoku? Brigitte Bardot *and* Salvador Dali? Ed himself was often novel. He had his own convent of Marist nuns up in Boston, prepared to pray for him every time he telephoned during a blackout or a strike. And once he told the nation: "Americans of Italian blood [are] getting a great wallop out of Nashua, Kentucky Derby favorite, as his granddaddy was the Italian horse Nearco, sire of Nasrullah. The Derby will be an all-paisan affair with Arcaro aboard Nashua." After which, *The New Yorker* was moved to comment: "You'll probably recall that Americans of Italian blood expressed the wallop they got from this state of affairs in scenes of wild excitement from coast to coast as soon as they had it straight in their minds whether it was Arcaro who was Nashua's granddaddy, with Nearco aboard, or vice versa."

For that matter, in the old Marlo Lewis days before Bob Precht took over, singers at the Sunday rehearsal used to wonder why Ray Bloch wasn't keeping time with their songs. This was because, on his headset, Bloch was listening instead to the radio broadcast of the New York Giants football game. The whole show was a novelty act.

Les Olympiades
(above), in 1966,
painted their semi-
naked bodies gold, and
then pretended, in
adagio, to be Greek
athletes posing for
Praxiteles.

———

One of the Three Kims
(opposite), in 1967,
uncovers a glitch in
their acrobatic act.

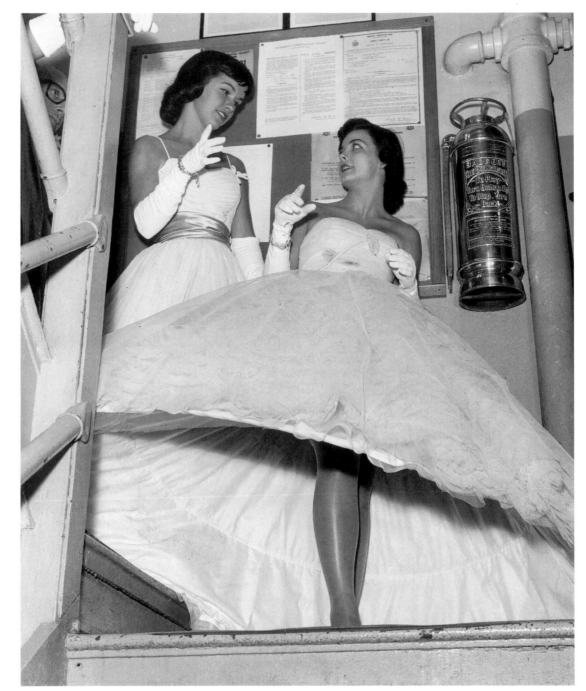

Opposite: Ed's devotion to Americana extended from Boy Scouts, drill teams, and college all-star football players to Native Americans, like these tribal representatives (top left) who performed ceremonial dances; the Texas Boys Choir (top right) in cowboy hats, in 1965; and, one time only in 1953, rope jumpers and baton twirlers (center left) from Des Moines, Iowa. In the middle of the Vietnam war in 1966, the United States Air Force Chorale (center right) sings a medley of battle songs while patriotic footage rolls. One of the Claytons (bottom left) whips his rope; Roy Rogers and Dale Evans (bottom right) both yodel and *Paint Your Wagon* in 1970.

Two of twenty-two contestants in the 1957 Miss America beauty pageant (above) wait their cues backstage before appearing on the Sullivan show in full formal regalia.

Overleaf: In 1969 Ed got bit by Victor the Bear while holding a chocolate-covered ice cream bar that was supposed to be Victor's reward for a job well done.

CLASSICAL

Prima ballerina Margot Fonteyn, before she became a Dame, first appeared on Ed's show in 1951.

Return with us now to the thrilling days of yesteryear, when television in its infancy was the lowbrow medium that brought us, for instance, Hopalong Cassidy, Buffalo Bob Smith, Howdy Doody, and Bishop Sheen. To a lowbrow, middlebrow looks highbrow. In order to feel good about itself, the middlebrow always includes some highbrow: with a certain amount of resentment, to be sure, but dutifully, too. Important people claim to like this higher culture, so maybe it's good for us. But these important people also looked a lot like snobs, imitating the manners of some imaginary class above them, in the way bohemians imitate the manners of the class below them. On Sullivan's Broadway, snobbery was against the rules. Still, nobody seemed to know exactly how one was supposed to feel about the opera singer who had to learn all those foreign languages, or the ballet dancer who ate like a bird and never had time for sex, or the longhair who played Chopin instead of Joplin. These serious people, so somehow *European*, obviously weren't in it for the big bucks and fast parties. They made you nervous.

Robert Merrill, equally
at home on the Met's
stage and on Ed's — and
at Yankee Stadium,
where his recorded "Star-
Spangled Banner" is still
heard before each
baseball game — sings an
opera medley in 1970.

They questioned your street values. So you slipped them something, and hoped they'd like you. About Ed, when he introduced these class acts, there was always an importuning and an insecurity. But, hey, his father had loved this stuff. And it was spectacle, wasn't it? And Ed was in the spectacle business, like everybody else on Broadway. By Ed Sullivan's middlebrow, with the help of a deal he made for first refusal on anything imported by the indefatigable promoter-impresario Sol Hurok, television would upwardly mobilize itself.

Besides, like the theater, the Metropolitan Opera House was just a few blocks away from his studio. Maybe as a byproduct of their tantrums and all that nineteenth-century Italian passion, divas in particular had always had the sort of star quality prized by the celebrity culture Ed was helping to create, even though he had to wait a few years for Maria Callas to glamorize opera the way Arnold Palmer glamorized golf. And so from the beginning of his TV show, we could expect to see someone like Roberta Peters — "the little Cinderella from the Bronx" — fresh from her front-page triumph as a walk-on Zerlina in *Don Giovanni*. In addition to those tonsils, Peters was a wonderful *story*, like the American Van Cliburn's surprise winning of the Tschaikovsky competition of

Richard Tucker (left) as
the heartbroken clown
in Leoncavallo's
Pagliacci in 1969.

Overleaf: Van Cliburn,
in 1961, performs
Chopin's *Polonaise* in a
Sullivan show "remote"
from the Sportpalast in
West Berlin.

pianists in Moscow, or a pubescent Itzhak Perlman discovered on the streets of Tel Aviv.

After Peters we got Marian Anderson, Eileen Farrell, Dorothy Kirsten, Anna Moffo, Patrice
Munsel, Birgit Nilsson, Lily Pons, Leontyne Price, Elisabeth Schwarzkopf, Beverly Sills, Risë Stevens,
Joan Sutherland, Renata Tebaldi, Helen Traubel. On hand to hulk at them were Franco Corelli
and Lauritz Melchior, Richard Tucker and Leonard Warren, Ezio Pinza and Cesare Siepi, Robert
Merrill and Jan Peerce. What, you may wonder, was in it for the Met, or for La Scala? After all,
they were permitted only snippets, an aria here and a chorus there, like Mozart's or Verdi's Greatest
Hits. And they had to put up with the usual indignities attendant on the electric circus: Late in his
life, all anybody wanted to hear from Jan Peerce was his rendition of "The Bluebird of Happiness";
Joan Sutherland had to appear on stage with Tanya the Elephant; and no one who witnessed it will
ever forget Risë Stevens singing "Cement Mixer (Put-ti, Put-ti)."

Well, there was money and publicity, and opera stars are mostly hams, and Beverly Sills went
on to direct the New York City Opera, and Robert Merrill would get to sing the national anthem
at every New York Yankees home game, and so Ed's show must have been a shrewd career move.

In her ninth of twelve appearances, Maria Neglia (above), in 1958, trifles on the violin with "Plink, Plank, Plunk." Discovered when he was twelve years old by Ed in Tel Aviv, Itzhak Perlman (below) made his first television appearance when he was thirteen and a half. He's a little older here, in 1964, in his third appearance on the show, playing Wieniawski's "Concerto No. 2."

In her first and only appearance on the show, in 1968, Kyung Wha Chung (above) breaks a string on her violin. There are no other violins available, so all she can do on live television is smile at Ed, for which he thanks her graciously. The ten Japanese children known as the Suzuki Violins (below) perform in 1966 and help introduce what went on to become one of the most successful music-teaching methods in this country.

Opposite: Another "scoop" for Ed, although the ratings were a great disappointment: Maria Callas, in 1956, sings the title role in the Metropolitan Opera's production of Puccini's *Tosca*.

Anna Moffo (top left), who appeared six times, sings "Je Veux Vivre" in 1962; Joan Sutherland (center left), in the fourth of six appearances, sings "Ardon Gli'incensi" in 1964.

Roberta Peters (top right), one of Ed's all-time favorites, with the crowd-pleaser "Laughing Song" in 1965. Leontyne Price (center right), in 1961, revolutionized the way we heard "The Lord's Prayer." Beverly Sills (bottom) appeared only once, in 1969, to sing a Donizetti aria, "O luce di quest'anima."

Franco Corelli and
Dorothy Kirsten in a
1966 duet from
Puccini's *La Bohème*.

Ed himself was a man of utmost dignity, yet for a good promotional cause he once allowed himself
to be photographed, for the cover of *Esquire*, in a Beatles wig.

It's also tempting to think of grand opera on the Sullivan show as the first music video, except that Ed over the years hardened in his firm opinion that the American public preferred seeing
the singers in evening clothes, rather than their costumes. Let's pause for a moment to consider this.
Is it true? It must be, because Ed said so, and who else would know? He was as good at reviewing
the public as, say, Pauline Kael was at reviewing movies. It was Kael who told us that "when opera
singers go into the movies, the baritones can act but the tenors can't."

In 1953, live from the stage at the Met, he telecast part of the last act of *Carmen* with Risë
Stevens and Richard Tucker, to approving reviews and audience acclaim. (So much for public television's higher-than-thou-brow patting of itself on the back for having been the first to do any such
thing twenty-four years later.) And in the mid-Fifties, Sullivan entered into a $100,000 deal with
Rudolf Bing at the Met. To five different famous operas, on five separate Sunday nights, Ed's show
promised to devote eighteen minutes each. The first of these Sundays was November 26, 1956,
and the first of the operas was *Tosca*, with Maria Callas making her television debut. This was Ed's
best shot, and it cost him six points off his average in the Trendex ratings. The second Sunday was
January 27, 1957, and the opera was *Madame Butterfly*, with Dorothy Kirsten, and Ed actually *lost*
his time period to the competition. Sullivan and Bing, two equally matched imperial egos, blamed
each other for the developing fiasco. By the third Sunday, March 10, a ruthless and desperate Ed had
cut *La Bohème* down to a four-minute duet by Renata Tebaldi and Richard Tucker. So much for grand
opera. Elvis had shown him another way. We hear a lot about what television has done to the attention span of the American public. We never hear anything about what the attention span of the
American public has done to television.

Enough tapping, please. Ballet was an easier sell than opera: sort of like baseball in tutus, and
you never saw a fat prima. *Nutcracker* belonged to everybody's childhood, and who among us could

Japan's classic Fujiwara
Opera Company
appears on Ed's stage
in 1956.

Roland Petit's Corps de
Ballet kick up their
heels in "España" in
1964.

possibly resist Moira Shearer in *The Red Shoes*? If Roberta Peters had been front-page in New York singing circles, the defection of a Rudolf Nureyev from the Soviet Union for the sake of his art was front-page all over the civilized world. And teaming him with Dame Margot Fonteyn was socko box office. Like the Met, the Joffrey and the New York City Ballet were just around the corner, Jerome Robbins was always available, San Francisco and Chicago sent their companies, and so did London and Florence, Hungary and Israel, Spain and Japan. And, of course, the Bolshoi was a smash — overrated, at least that first company they sent us, but a smash. From Agnes DeMille to Maya Plisetskaya, nobody on commercial television was ever better for serious dance than Ed Sullivan, and nowhere else could you count on seeing it, except perhaps on *Omnibus*.

Because of all he did for dance, Ed may be forgiven for what he didn't do for serious art — Salvador Dali and Peter Max would not change the way we saw the world. And he wasn't a whole lot better on serious poetry. We did get a little Dylan Thomas, because Richard Burton insisted on reading it when the Welsh vapors took him, as Charles Laughton insisted on reading the Bible. Carl Sandburg doesn't count, because he was reading Lincoln's letters. Ogden Nash at least knew he was funny, whereas Rod McKuen didn't. Serious music was a happier story. While we could

Edward Villella, in the first of eight appearances, with Patricia McBride in 1966.

have heard some on the *Bell Telephone* and *Firestone* hours or whenever NBC let Toscanini rip, and there is a very real question as to whether Arthur Fiedler and André Kostelanetz ought to be mentioned at all in highbrow company, Sullivan's was the only mass-market show to welcome classical piano; the violin and flute; the French horn, the cello, the harp, and the stray Yehudi Menuhin, so long as the soloist was somehow famous somewhere else, like Andrés Segovia, a kind of Mickey Mantle of the guitar.

And when Ed went away, who would step in to hold the middle of that brow? Except for occasional White House galas, and on CBS with Charles Kuralt Sunday mornings, opera's disappeared from network television. Ballet is something that happens only on public television, more often than not during Pledge Week; or on Bravo, the premium cable service for those determined to improve themselves. Symphony orchestras, like local dance troupes and regional theaters and modern jazz quartets, have to be subsidized by the federal government or philanthropized by the oil companies. Even our libraries are now closed after dark. Somewhere along the line to junk bonds, buy-outs, and hostile takeovers, the middlebrows stopped trying harder — and America settled for, or maybe even turned into, a greed-head musical comedy.

Villella again (above),
from *Giselle* in 1965.

Opposite: Maya
Plisetskaya, in 1962, as
a "Swan" to die for.

Fresh from his Soviet
defection, Rudolf
Nureyev performs
Swan Lake with
Margot Fonteyn
(above) in 1965.

Opposite: Helped by his
exposure on the
Sullivan shows,
Nureyev, here in 1965
dancing "Gayane,"
became the first male
ballet superstar in
America.

Sports

Pro basketball center and scoring champ Wilt Chamberlain looks down on Ed and *Wizard of Oz* Munchkin Billy Barty, in 1962.

It was a guy thing — even though Babe Didrikson Zaharias and Knute Rockne's widow did crash the party three times, and Sonja Henie and Florence Chadwick once, and we won't count the baseball Yankee wives because this was before the players, like Fritz Peterson and Mike Kekich, started swapping them.

But long before Ed Sullivan had known or written about anything else in this world, before women and nightclubs and lamb chops and Renoir, he'd been a sport: athlete, reporter, fan, and benefactor. His first big interview after high school was of Babe Ruth. His first big interview in New York was of Jack Dempsey. His first byline in journalism's big leagues was on a dog-show story. His first philanthropic project was a destitute boxer, Johnny Dundee. When he was no longer young enough to stay out all night and play golf at dawn, he bought some horses of his own to race. So he liked to hang out with the guys — the athletes, the champions — and, naturally, he wanted them on his show, especially if they were down on their luck and could use a thousand bucks to stand

Yankee baseball great Mickey Mantle, another of Ed's favorites, explained on the Sullivan show the reasons for his retirement from the game. Here, in 1960, he gives Ed batting tips.

up in the audience. In the fires of his admiration, they would glow again. And in those long decades before Robert Bly, all of them might bond, as if CBS were a drum.

Look at their faces. Not the Hungarian Olympic Team, nor the Finnish Women's Gymnasts, but the guys. Like the baseball players: Hank Aaron, Yogi Berra, Ken Boyer, Lou Brock, Roy Campanella, Don Drysdale, Whitey Ford, Bob Gibson, Gil Hodges, Roger Maris, Willie Mays, Gil McDougald, Stan Musial, Don Newcombe, Dusty Rhodes, Phil Rizzuto, Jackie Robinson, Duke Snider, Ted Williams, and Carl Yastrzemski. Not quite so many boxers, all but one of them heavyweights: Cassius Clay (before and after he became Ali), Jack Dempsey, Joe Frazier, Sonny Liston, Joe Louis, Rocky Marciano, Floyd Patterson, Sugar Ray Robinson. As many golfers: Billy Casper, Jr., Ben Hogan, Byron Nelson, Arnold Palmer, Gary Player, Chi Chi Rodriguez, Sam Snead, and Babe D-Z. Not so many football players, if we don't count mass meetings of the Baltimore Colts and the college all-star teams: Frank Gifford, Ron Mix, Roger Staubach, Fran Tarkenton, Johnny Unitas. In the winner's circle: sixteen jockeys, from Eddie Arcaro to Angel Valenzuela, though we musn't forget the group of riders that showed up in 1953 dressed in top hat and tails doing the soft shoe. Only a few basketball players, not counting the Globetrotters: Bob Cousy and Lew Alcindor and Wilt Chamberlain, who hadn't yet written of his 20,000 one-night stands. On the ice, Dick Button. At the billiard table, Willie Mosconi. All-purpose: Jesse Owens and Jim Thorpe. All wet: Johnny Weissmuller and Esther Williams.

Ed takes it on the chin from Ezzard Charles (left) and Rocky Marciano (right) as golfer Ed Furgol looks on.

Go ahead, he told the competition. An hour later, Hogan was on the phone: "They had no authority to call you. Your offer was a thousand dollars win, lose, or draw. That meant more to me than any of the offers I got since I won. If you still want me for a grand, I'm not appearing on any other show."

But Ed's guys were before the age of jet-propelled sneakers and charging for autographs. When Ed first went on the air, there were hardly any baseball games except at parks and on the radio. Nobody cared about pro football. Not even public television carried tennis. Who could possibly have imagined Congress legislating the inalienable right of the American male to see his professional football team on television *every* Sunday? Or World Series baseball games played at night in subfreezing mid-October temperatures, for the prime-time ratings? Or the natural rhythms of basketball and hockey interrupted solely for the purpose of commercial messages? Or tie-breakers so tennis won't go on forever into the next regularly scheduled program? Or cable systems developed to feed home-town athletic contests into bars and other bunkers of the betting action? Or franchises shifting cities in search of a bigger television market or a lucrative pay-TV deal? Or whole leagues shutting down because they can't get a network contract?

Big bad heavyweight boxer Sonny Liston needs some help from singer Eddie Fisher to test Ed's chin (right) in 1962.

Opposite: Though champion of the world in 1970, Muhammad Ali appears on the Sullivan show as a Broadway musical star, who grew a full beard for his role in *Buck White,* in which he sang "We Came in Chains."

Overleaf: Right here on our stage in 1964, Meadowlark Lemon and the Harlem Globetrotters, who never lost a basketball game.

In retrospect, sports seem made for television. Some sports, in fact, have been invented *just* for television: tennis challenge matches, a World Series of golf, punt-pass-and-kick contests, basketball-dunking competitions. And *ABC's Wide World of Sports* was without a doubt the Sullivan show of the Sweat Set: demolition derbies, world land-speed records, computerized prizefights, Japanese all-star games, target diving, barrel jumping, kick boxing, ice boating, and the annual Duke Kahanamoku surfing classic.

At its most compelling, TV promises that anything can happen next and when it does, we'll see it, we will be the first to know. News and sports are the principal sources of these brutal and decisive moments, instants of the absolute. But news has a way of happening at inconvenient times and places, without any warning to a camera crew; and even then, it's seldom decisive, or visually dramatic. The nice thing about a game is that you know in advance where and when it will be played, and at some point it's over, and somebody or other can be seen to have won or lost. Into its doldrums, moreover, the tekkies can insert their instant replays, the slo-mo and split screen and freeze frame. And the "color analysts" will tell us what we saw as if it were as complicated as an invasion of Panama or a deconstruction from the French.

This is the football influence, on sportscasting and on television news. The glorification of pig-kick has made us conceive of our daily lives as something essentially brutish: a long bomb, a red-dog blitz, a crackback block, a quarterback sack, and sudden death in overtime. Whereas in Ed's day, before the whole world turned into hectic television, there was a kinder and gentler mix of metaphors, and they were baseball's, and they spoke of *extra innings*, instead of sudden death, the *slow curve* and the *no-hitter*, the *intentional walk* and the home-run *trot*. What about *rain delay*? And most beautiful of all . . . *stealing home*.

Ed, in 1964, with Jim Brown (far left), Cleveland Browns running back, who later went out to Hollywood; Ed, in 1968, with Joe Namath (left), New York Jets quarterback, who would later go on to win the Super Bowl and then sell panty hose in television commercials.

In 1956, as in most years, the All-Star Team of American college football players made a guest appearance on Ed's stage. Here, they seem to be looking for somebody's fumble.

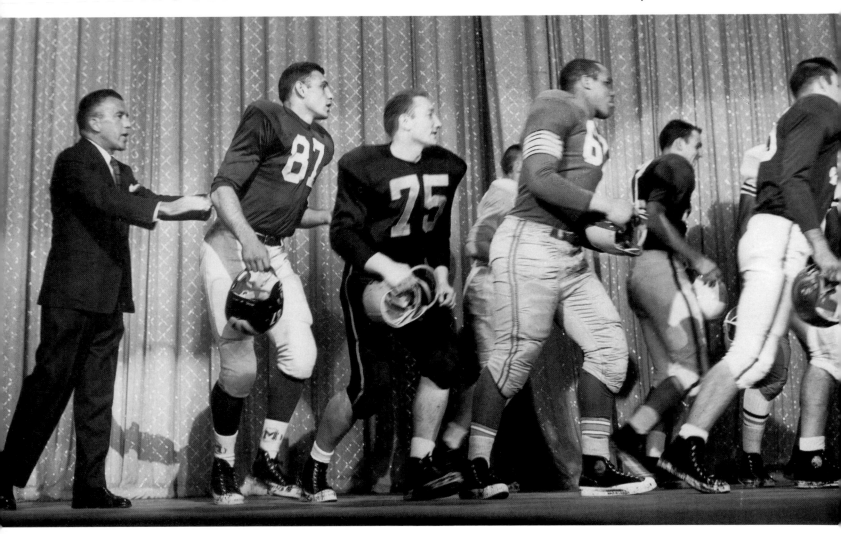

BROADWAY

Ed and Noël Coward,
the recently knighted
British actor,
playwright, tunesmith,
and wit, for a *Brief
Encounter* in 1957.

Perhaps you knew, as most of the country did, that Helen Hayes was mourning her dead daughter, Mary MacArthur, when she went on the Sullivan show to do a scene from *Victoria Regina*. The scene she chose was Victoria's return to the palace, after a long day's ride through London. She is asked if she is tired. She says she had been, at one point, when rough workingmen broke through a thin police line and rushed her carriage. Had they been anarchists? But the roughest of them called out to her, "Go it, Old Girl; you've done it well." And at curtain call, Hayes said: "Someday I'll be making my last appearance. I've lived a singularly blessed life. I've done the things I've loved best with the people I've loved most, the people of the theater. Perhaps before I make my last exit from the stage, you of the American audience, who have been so kind to me, may feel impelled to call out, 'Go it, Old Girl; you've done it well.'"

Along with Josh Logan's impromptu plea for a better understanding of mental illness, this was one of Ed's favorite moments in the history of the show. And there were many to choose from

When Ed did a salute to Broadway producer and director Josh Logan in 1953, Logan asked him for time to speak impromptu about his own hospitalization for mental illness, a special moment in the history of the show.

that came straight from Broadway to his stage and our homes, to switch on language like a light. Just imagine: Julie Harris on the lap of Ethel Waters, while Brandon de Wilde leaned on both of them in Carson McCullers's *Member of the Wedding*. Or Richard Burton as sober as he ever got, with Julie Andrews in a scene from *Camelot*. Or Judith Anderson, the world's most difficult mother, in a Robinson Jeffers adaptation of Euripides's *Medea*. Or Eva Le Gallienne, whom Chekhov must have had in mind when he wrote *The Cherry Orchard*. Or half the cast of Bernstein's *West Side Story* and everybody who was anybody in the tribe of *Hair*.

From the beginning, with Rodgers and Hammerstein as unpaid guests on the very first *Toast of the Town*, Sullivan and the legitimate theater he covered for his column were allies. As early as 1950, back to back on Sunday nights, he brought *Member of the Wedding* to television, black and white together, followed by a bit of the Broadway revival of Erskine Caldwell's *Tobacco Road*. Selections from George Gershwin's *Of Thee I Sing* and Frank Loesser's *Guys and Dolls* were soon to come. By 1952 Ed was even saving plays. The musical comedy *Wish You Were Here* was dead in the summer humidity until the producer sent its stars to rescue it on Sullivan. Ed even had one of the show's first sets constructed to accommodate those stars, a replica of a swimming pool, with mirrors to simulate depth. The next day lines formed early at the theater, the closing notice came down, and *Wish You Were Here* lasted 587 additional performances.

One more example: *All the Way Home* opened in November 1960, to favorable reviews and a disappointing box office. With $882 in the second-night till, producer Arthur Cantor posted a closing notice, but asked Ed to introduce two cast members from his audience that Sunday night. Ed did better; he endorsed the play and told everybody they ought to buy tickets. Two hours after the Belasco box office opened the Monday after, $2,000 worth of tickets had been sold, with long lines still waiting. The following June, *All the Way Home* won a Pulitzer Prize.

But if Ed was good for Broadway, Broadway was also good for Ed. Because he was, as one of his biographers put it, an "unstar," he didn't need to build his variety hour around talents compatible with his own, to appear like Milton Berle in every skit (which would have been a trial for, say, Judith Anderson). His ace in the hole during the ferocious competition with the *Colgate Comedy Hour*

Jessica Tandy and
Hume Cronyn (left), in
1951, with a scene from
The Fourposter.

———

Overleaf: Anthony
Newley belts out
"Nothing Can Stop Me
Now!" and "Who Can
I Turn To?" from the
Broadway musical
*The Roar of the
Greasepaint, the Smell
of the Crowd,* in 1965;
Yul Brynner, in 1951,
rehearsing "Is a
Puzzlement" from *The
King and I.*

Audrey Hepburn and
Rex Harrison in a 1952
scene from *Anne of a
Thousand Days.*

Pearl Bailey in a scene from the 1967 all-black Broadway production of *Hello, Dolly!*

Gwen Verdon doing "If My Friends Could See Me Now" from *Sweet Charity,* a routine personally choreographed by Sullivan part-timer Bob Fosse in 1967.

Joel Grey and his wanton nightclub women, in 1969, sing a song against the Nazis in *Cabaret*.

The tribe from *Hair* let the sun shine in, also in 1969.

Onstage with Ethel
Waters in 1949. When
she appeared the next
year in a mixed-race
segment of *Member of
the Wedding,* some
members of the
audience were shocked.

Alec Guinness (top) in 1964 as the self-destructive Welsh poet Dylan Thomas, from the Broadway play *Dylan.* Carol Lawrence (below), famous overnight as Maria in *West Side Story,* appeared on the show seventeen times. In 1957, she's singing "It Might as Well Be Spring."

Overleaf: Sammy Davis, Jr., irrepressible as usual, whips the stage into shape with *Golden Boy* in 1964.

Richard Kiley (right) in need of a windmill in *Man of La Mancha.*

was all that talent down the block, young and able or tried and true, and almost always available for Sunday morning rehearsals of a little this and a little that from *Carousel* and *Camelot,* from *My Fair Lady* and from *Auntie Mame.* It was on Sullivan's show that most of the country first heard of Cornelia Otis Skinner and where Yul Brynner on a visit from *The King and I* first became an icon of the popular culture (and, incidentally, an offense to the sensibilities of Thailand, where the movie's still banned). And where else till their musicals were turned into movies could you see Ethel Merman, or Carol Channing, or Gwen Verdon as engineered by Bob Fosse?

We saw Jason Robards and George Grizzard in a bit of *The Disenchanted;* Tony Roberts and Lou Jacobi in *Don't Drink the Water;* Shirley Booth and Al Freeman in *Lilies of the Field;* Henry Fonda, James Cagney, and Jack Lemmon in *Mister Roberts;* Melvyn Douglas in *Spofford* and Vivien Leigh in *Tovarich;* Paul Newman in *This Is the Army* and James Earl Jones in *The Great White Hope.* After *Guys and Dolls,* as if at a benefit for one of the more popular diseases, all the Broadway musicals showed up: *Auntie Mame, The Boyfriend, Brigadoon, Bye Bye Birdie, Cabaret, Camelot, Carousel, Fiddler on the Roof, Flower Drum Song, Gypsy, Hello, Dolly!, Kiss Me, Kate, Oklahoma!, Paint Your Wagon, The Pajama Game, Show Boat, South Pacific, Wonderful Town,* and *Zorba.* Which meant that Julie Andrews, Joel Grey, Chita Rivera, Theodore Bikel, Barbra Streisand, Richard Burton, Gertrude Lawrence, Jerry Orbach, Mary Martin, Phil Silvers, Elaine Stritch, Sammy Davis, Jr., Tammy Grimes, Stanley Holloway, Bernadette Peters, and Herschel Bernardi also showed, and sang and danced.

Anything went and everybody got a kick out of Ed's chat with composer Cole Porter (near right) in 1952; Ed devoted a whole show in 1957 to Alan Jay Lerner and Frederick Loewe (far right), the lyricist-composer team that gave us *Brigadoon*, *Paint Your Wagon*, and *My Fair Lady*.

"There are no people like show people.

So how about a nice hand for all of them."

Ed did another show in 1962 for Richard Rodgers (above), who wrote *South Pacific* and *The King and I*. Ira Gershwin (center), shown here in 1964, wrote the words to his brother George's music in *Funny Face* and *Strike Up the Band*. By 1951, Oscar Hammerstein (right) had already collaborated with Rodgers on such Broadway hits as *Oklahoma!* and *Carousel*.

Ed threw a birthday party for the composer of "Me and My Gal" and "White Christmas" in 1966. Irving Berlin must have enjoyed it; he lived on to age 101.

Remember that all the little theaters in all the smaller cities of the nation had yet to be built. Repertory was a dream. Not even the universities had got into the sort of stage business that can be found on campuses everywhere today — from the Yale Dramat in New Haven to the Loeb at Harvard. Where else was there to go if you were hungry for actors with the dramatic literature at their fingertips? Sooner or later, they'd all drop by the Sullivan show, almost at random: Bert Lahr and Eileen Heckart; Rex Harrison and Lilli Palmer; Alfred Lunt and Lynn Fontanne; Hume Cronyn and Jessica Tandy; James Mason and Celeste Holm; Fredric March and Kim Stanley. And as they had been and would be at the theater, they were unrepentantly live. This is always television at its best, when anything can happen, but the people to whom it will happen are professionals, and so there will be surprise and grace, like jazz and basketball.

So Lunt does scenes from *Idiot's Delight* and *There Shall Be No Night*. And not only will Carl Sandburg show up to read from Lincoln's letters, but we will also get Abe himself, in the considerable person of Raymond Massey, doing the farewell address from Robert E. Sherwood's *Abe Lincoln in Illinois*, complete with ten stagehands pulling an iron horse. This is much more exciting than having to sit through Hedy Lamarr's rendition of "Rock-a-Bye Baby."

Richard Burton and Julie Andrews, in 1961, enjoy the view from *Camelot*. This appearance on the Sullivan show is the only visual record remaining of Burton's Tony-winning performance in the blockbuster Broadway musical.

Stanley Holloway (left), from *My Fair Lady* in 1957, confesses to "a little bit of luck."

Opposite: Dame Judith Anderson, in 1966, as *Elizabeth the Queen*.

And something else to remember, because the Sullivan show fed so on these talents and energies: Although it has certainly done significant damage to newspapers in this country, television didn't kill movies, which seem to be killing themselves with their preposterous budgets; and it didn't kill books, of which 50,000 new ones are published each year; and it didn't kill Broadway, which is always sickly anyway. What Sullivan's television did for Broadway was acquaint the rest of the country with the fact that it was still alive. Like those experiments in the workplace environment in Hawthorne, New York, where every change — from new colors on the walls to different music on the sound system to rearrangements of the desks — improved productivity; like the market testing in Wichita, Kansas, of beer kegs for home refrigerators that upped the sale of every kind of beer from bottles and cans to the tap at the bar . . . attention wakes up everybody, makes them feel wanted. So what if all we got were morsels? Morsels make you hungry. So what if we never saw Beckett or Pinter? Ed wasn't in business to frighten his audience; he just wanted us to clap our hands, and week after week we found ourselves willing to believe again in every sort of Tinker Bell.

ROCK AND ROLL

Two of the biggest acts in rock and roll history appeared on Ed's show: Elvis (here, in 1956) and the Beatles (1964).

Elvis wasn't the first rocker on the Sullivan show. In late 1955, Ed, always eager to acknowledge talented black musicians, put together a tribute to popular R&B artists of the period, including LaVern Baker, Billy Ward and the Dominoes, and upcoming Bo Diddley, who resisted Ed's command to sing "Sixteen Tons" and substituted his own hit song, conveniently called "Bo Diddley." But when Ed was offered Presley a year later, at a bargain basement price of $5,000, he passed. "I hooted at that kind of money," he recalled, "because this was a youngster apparently known only in the South."

But a terrible thing happened to Ed, on his way to the Trendex ratings the following July. After brief appearances on the Milton Berle and Tommy Dorsey programs, Elvis came on directly opposite Sullivan one Sunday night, on the brand-new *Steve Allen Show*. The Monday news was Ed, 14.8; Elvis, 20.2. To Allen Ed sent a gracious telegram: STEVEN PRESLEY ALLEN, NBC TV, NEW YORK CITY. STINKER. LOVE AND KISSES. ED SULLIVAN. To a reporter who called for a reaction, however, Ed said, "I don't think Elvis Presley is fit for family viewing," though *some* people will do anything for ratings.

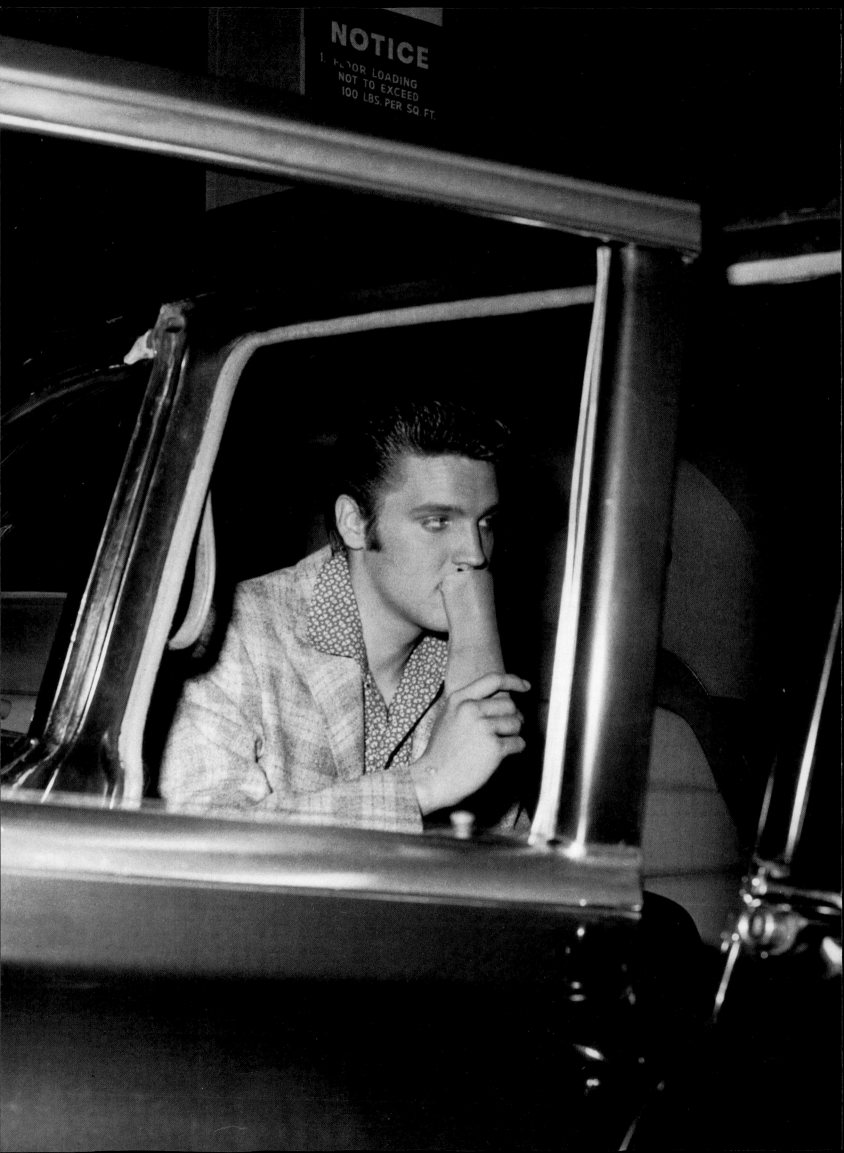

Elvis arrives for a rehearsal at Television City in Hollywood in 1956 when he was simultaneously filming *Loving You.* His live appearance on the Sullivan show, opening the Fall 1956 season, was the publicity event of the year. Producer Marlo Lewis flew to California to oversee the camera work. In New York, Charles Laughton was the substitute master of ceremonies, when Ed was in the hospital recovering from his automobile accident. These previously unpublished photographs were taken during the Hollywood rehearsal. Four months later, Elvis would appear on Ed's show for the third and final time, shot from the waist up only.

Just three hours later, though, he was on the phone with Elvis's manager Colonel Tom Parker and they struck a $50,000 deal for three appearances, and — contrary to whatever you may think you remember — when Elvis showed up on Sullivan for the first of those appearances, September 9, 1956, we saw all of him. What many people forget is that we never saw Ed. A month earlier Ed had been in a near-fatal automobile accident while driving to his Connecticut farm. While he was recovering in the hospital, producer Marlo Lewis flew to Hollywood to take over the control room, and it was Charles Laughton, subbing for the injured Ed, who introduced "Elvin" Presley to the nation. And everybody who was alive that night will tell you they were watching.

The second appearance, a month later, also gave us a full-bodied Elvis, albeit with subdued lighting and long overhead lenses and side-angle camera work. At least — unlike Johnnie Ray, "The Little White Cloud That Cried" — Elvis hadn't foamed at the mouth. But by the third appearance — January 6, 1957 — after having been burned in effigy in St. Louis, and hanged in effigy in Nashville, and banned, or at least his lower-body movements, in the state of Florida, a full-frontal Elvis suddenly seemed provocative. And Sullivan's staff decided that all America should see of Elvis that night was his torso, his guitar, his sideburns, and those sleepy eyes full of working-class whiteboy crossover dreams.

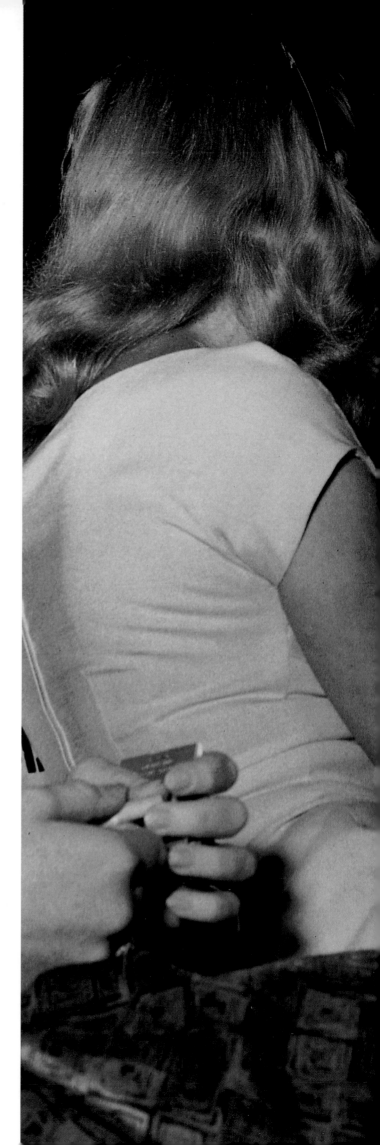

"I want to say to Elvis and the country that this is a real decent, fine boy. We want to say that we've never had a pleasanter experience on our show with a big name than we've had with you. You're thoroughly all right.**"**

New Orleans musician Fats Domino was one of many black recording artists who were singing rock and roll long before any of the white boys got into the act. Here he is in 1962, with "Let the Four Winds Blow."

These men knew how to make it happen. James Brown (right), the Godfather of Soul, sings a medley of his hits, including "Please Please Please," in 1966. You couldn't get much smoother than Sam Cooke (below left), in 1957, singing "You Send Me."

One of the most hypnotic performers of all time, Jackie Wilson sings "That's Why" in 1962.

By then Elvis was on his way to Hollywood and the movies and could easily have been making $50,000 a single shot, but Parker honored their contract. Besides, Ed had decided to like the boy. He'd seen him at a CBS press conference where a reporter asked him if he was embarrassed when "silly little girls" kissed his new white Cadillac, and Elvis had replied, "Well, ma'am, if it hadn't been for what you call these silly little girls, I wouldn't have that white Cadillac." This was something Ed could understand, like Trendex and the Delmonico.

But did any of us understand at the time what else was going on? Elvis not only opened the gates of the Sullivan show to all the barbarian rock hordes yet to come; he also opened locked doors — to the attic, the basement, and the bedroom — of the Eisenhower culture.

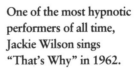

In 1957, Buddy Holly
and the Crickets
(above) sing "Peggy
Sue" in one of their rare
television appearances;
fifteen-year-old Frankie
Lymon (below),
without the Teenagers,
sings his only solo hit,
"Goody Goody."

Opposite: Also in 1957,
Bill Haley and His
Comets perform "Forty
Cups of Coffee" on Ed's
stage. Their "Rock
Around the Clock,"
selling twenty-five
million copies in 1955,
was the first big
crossover rock hit.
When it appeared in the
movie *The Blackboard
Jungle,* it was
immediately obvious to
parents that rock and
roll caused juvenile
delinquency.

What's Chubby
Checker doing in 1961?
The twist, of course, in
front of forty million
Americans, after which
the dance craze went
international and
peppermint.

Lolita wants, Sullivan gets," he sat down with Beatles' manager Brian Epstein and they cut a deal for three shows in 1964 for $10,000. This was all part of a carefully orchestrated plan by Epstein, who had waited until the Beatles were at the top of the U.K. charts in the fall of 1963 to begin his siege of America. The Beatles might have sold eleven million records worldwide, but not enough of them in the United States. Epstein was determined to change all that. By February the American public was ready, and Epstein, who was conspiring with Capitol Records on a publicity firestorm for "I Want to Hold Your Hand," brought the boys over. It turned out to be a very good idea. After a congratulatory telegram from Elvis, in oddly Edwardian suits, with freshly laundered moptops, on their very best behavior, the Beatles were watched by almost seventy-four million Americans.

But not before they'd charmed reporters at Kennedy Airport. (Question: "How do you find America?" Ringo: "Turn left at Greenland.") And partied at the Plaza. (Which next time would refuse them room at the inn, so Sullivan had to slip them into the Warwick.) And fought their way from their dressing room through a thicket of Leonard Bernstein and his daughters. (Fifty thousand people, including Jack Paar's daughter Randy, wanted tickets to a theater that sat 728.) From which they were off, first to Carnegie Hall, and then to Washington, D.C. and Miami, for their second Sullivan, and the second biggest ratings victory in the show's history, the first Beatles appearance being the only bigger triumph. While the Beatles were on the air, incidentally, there seems to have been no crime at all in the city of New York, at least on the streets.

The Beach Boys (left) sing "I Get Around" in 1964 with Brian Wilson still at the wheel.

Opposite: Bob Dylan, seen here in rehearsal, was supposed to sing "Talkin' John Birch Society Blues" in 1963, but CBS censors wouldn't let him. He refused to change songs and walked off the Sullivan show, never to return.

Ed's enthusiasm for Motown, combined with Motown founder Berry Gordy's ingenuity in timing the release of many of his groups' singles to coincide with their appearances on Sullivan's show, helped make the sound an amazing success throughout America. Here, in 1966, the Four Tops (right) sing one of their hits, "I Can't Help Myself (Sugar Pie, Honey Bunch)";

Martha and the Vandellas (center left) encourage "Dancing in the Street" on Ed's stage in 1965; a 1968 medley of Smokey Robinson and the Miracles (center right) featured "I Second That Emotion"; the Temptations (bottom left), in 1969, celebrate "September in the Rain"; Gladys Knight and the Pips (bottom right) give us "I Heard It Through the Grapevine" in 1968.

In 1964, "Little" Stevie
Wonder with harmonica
performs his first hit,
"Fingertips, Pt. 2."

The Jackson 5 perform
"I Want You Back"
and "The Love You
Save" in 1969, before
Michael traded in his
purple hat for a white
glove.

In their fifteen times on the Sullivan show, the Supremes sang their twelve biggest hits — including "Baby Love," "Come See About Me," "Stop! In the Name of Love," "I Hear a Symphony," and "Love Child." During that time Florence Ballard (far left) was replaced by Cindy Birdsong (far right, opposite), and the group became Diana Ross and the Supremes. In 1970 Diana Ross emerged as a solo superstar.

In all, the Beatles appeared ten times on Sullivan (including seven taped performances), compared to six times for the Stones, six for the Animals, and seven for Jackie Wilson. Except for the Dave Clark Five (twelve times), not a single rock group ever got up to the Louis Armstrong level (eighteen), much less posed a threat to Pearl Bailey (twenty-three) or Connie Francis (twenty-six) or Teresa Brewer (thirty-one) or, impossibly, Roberta Peters (forty-one). Ike and Tina Turner, Janis Joplin, Jefferson Airplane, Roy Orbison, Gene Vincent, Simon and Garfunkel, and Marvin Gaye happened by just once. Twos included Blood, Sweat and Tears, the Beach Boys, Bill Haley and His Comets, James Brown, Stevie Wonder, Ray Charles, Sam Cooke, Chubby Checker, Creedence Clearwater Revival, Fats Domino, Buddy Holly, and Vanilla Fudge. As for the threes: Herman's Hermits, Lovin' Spoonful, and the Mamas and the Papas.

ROCK AND ROLL

Opposite: In 1966, before they became a bridge over troubled waters, Simon and Garfunkel told us "I Am a Rock."

Behind Mick Jagger, as the Rolling Stones (top) do "Ruby Tuesday" in 1967, is Brian Jones, in white hat, with flute. Jones also played around with guitars and sitars. Legendary guitarist B.B. King (above) plays the blues, including "The Thrill Is Gone."

Overleaf: During a tempestuous rehearsal, Jim Morrison of the Doors promised Sullivan executives he would not sing the drug-insinuating word "higher" in their song "Light My Fire." Surprise, surprise, Morrison broke his word. It was the Doors' one and only appearance.

Sonny and Cher (above) sing "I Got You Babe" in 1965, before she became a Bad Girl and he was elected mayor of Palm Springs. José Feliciano (left), introduced as "He's blind — and he's Puerto Rican!" by an enthusiastic Ed, plays "Flight of the Bumble Bee" in 1966.

The Mamas and the Papas, in one of three appearances on the Sullivan show, sing "Dedicated to the One I Love" in 1967. The group used to bring Ed flowers and beads, and would announce their periodic breakups and reconciliations on his stage.

By the time rock got to Sullivan, the world was changing and so was television, and not, so far as he could see, exactly for the better. He *loved* Motown, especially the Supremes, in whom he seems to have found an imaginary amalgam of gospel and Tin Pan Alley. The Beatles, he just *liked*. But their fans frightened him. Once the Beatles had gone, he wouldn't let anybody into the theater under age eighteen without a parent or guardian. That didn't stop fans of the Stones, of course, from forcing Mick Jagger through a plate-glass window outside the studio in 1967. And the worst sign of the apocalypse was later that same year, when Herman's Hermits came to town. A high school student on a press pass had hung around backstage, then left by the stage door to be mistaken for a Hermit. A mob tore at his clothes. Fighting free into street traffic, he was killed by a passing car. To have died for Herman's Hermits . . . What was wrong with these people, that they couldn't behave themselves when Ed was *preventing* Robert Merrill?

Opposite: Janis Joplin only appeared once, in 1969, but everyone who saw her never forgot how she sang "Raise Your Hand" and "Maybe, Maybe, Maybe."

Overleaf: Tina Turner in 1970, before she split with Ike, doing "Proud Mary" and other perpetual-motion favorites with the Ikettes.

Richie Havens (above), in 1969, sings "High Flying Bird."

What was wrong was that his audience, in the studio and at home, had divided against itself. Parents and children not only watched different television in different rooms, but they seemed to live on different planets, with different gravities: moons like Selma and Saigon. Pop music was no longer harmless or edifying. For every Woodstock there seemed, alas, an Altamont. Much later, in her novel of the Sixties, *Tripmaster Monkey*, Maxine Hong Kingston wondered, "What if Chubby Checker does not mean us well? What if Chubby Checker is up to no good?"

The Doors, for instance, did not mean Ed well. They were supposed to be on more than once. But when they were asked in rehearsal to remove from their rendition of "Light My Fire" the provocative word "higher" with its implicit endorsement of altered states, by chemicals other than alcohol or nicotine, the Doors pretended they would, but didn't. Told, then, that they would never appear on the show again, Jim Morrison explained: "Hey, man, we just *did* the Sullivan show."

Elvis, the Beatles, and the Doors signified the confusion to come of politics and culture. The juvenile delinquents had their own tribal music and it wasn't "Sentimental Journey." Children of Sullivan, and of *Gilligan's Island*, flower-smoking media-Apaches like Abbie Hoffman (that Dennis the Menace who preferred to overthrow the government by means of bubble gum, "but I'm beginning to have my doubts") and Jerry Rubin (that poisoned Twinkie who declared, "Sirhan Sirhan is a Yippie!") took over campuses and parks, the Stock Exchange and the Evening News.

A nomadic society like America may need television as a sort of Big Neighbor, like Uncle Ed; a Mission Control and message center for integrating the disrelated; an electronic Elmer's Glue-All, where we go for moonshots and Super Bowls. But what we were seeing instead were dead Kennedys, dead Kings, Chicago, and My Lai. Perhaps it wasn't only illness that made Ed look tired, even stupefied, toward the end: Where was the coherence? The coherence was gone.

Ed and the Beatles, in
February 1964. After
their first appearance
on his show, the Fab
Four went to
Washington, D.C., for
their first live concert in
the United States, and
then to Miami, where
they bunked at the
Fontainebleau Hotel,
waterskied for the first
time, and celebrated
another ratings triumph
on the Sullivan show.

Toast of the Town

For nearly a quarter-century the greatest stars visited Ed, from Humphrey Bogart (top), for whom Ed used to be mistaken in his younger days, shown here in 1951, to a young Elizabeth Taylor (bottom), shown here publicizing her 1954 film *The Last Time I Saw Paris.*

Good buddy Jack Benny, who appeared on the show eleven times and whom Ed claimed to have "discovered" on his radio show, drop-deadpans in 1967.

Ed was an impresario, not a journalist. He wanted to give the American public what the American public wanted to get. Crucial to his success was his Vulcan mindmeld with the audience. Almost alone among early television performers, he could hardly wait to consult his Trendex or, later, his Nielsen rating; he was the first professional in a nursery school of amateurs. If Elvis was socko on *Steve Allen,* Ed bought three of him. When an arrangement with the Met cost him ratings points, that was the end of too much opera. He may have had no use for rock music, and still less for the hysterical teenagers it drew to his theater, but with the Beatles and the Stones he could sell more pairs of eyes to the advertising agencies than anybody else on network TV.

In this, of course, he perfectly anticipated the very market researchers and their network executive groupies who would ultimately decide, in 1971, that he had had his day. By the end of the Sixties there were twenty variety shows on television. And the mind of the public had itself frag-

Lena Horne (left), who appeared on television for the first time on Ed's show in 1948, sings in 1957 a medley of "It's Love," "One for My Baby (and One More for the Road)," and "It's All Right With Me."

Opposite: Jazz great Ella Fitzgerald was a regular on the program, either singing alone, or with Duke Ellington, or with Sammy Davis, Jr. In 1957 she sang "Lady Be Good," and as always she was perfect.

mented. With more than one set in most American homes, young and old no longer sat down together to watch the same program. Nor was New York any longer the ptolemaic center of the entertainment universe. But what a long day it had been.

Starting in 1951, long before there were "life-styles" of the rich and famous, there were "biographies" of them on Sullivan's show. When Ed decided as a ratings gimmick to devote entire programs to the likes of Bea Lillie, Cole Porter, Sophie Tucker, Bert Lahr, and Walt Disney, he inadvertently invented the television "spectacular," by which television graduated from vaudeville, from radio, from Broadway, into a humming ether all its own. Some of the best moments on Sullivan's Sunday nights emerged from these "biographies," including Oscar Hammerstein's plaintive rendition of "The Last Time I Saw Paris," and the teaming up of Sophie Tucker with the Ink Spots. But the finest moment may have been in 1953, when Joshua Logan, having heard all those nice things said about him, threw away his script.

Several weeks before an hour-long television tribute to the director of *Bus Stop, Picnic,* and *South Pacific,* Logan told Sullivan that he wanted to talk about his own nervous breakdown, his stay in a sanitarium, and his recovery. Sullivan and Logan's friends dissuaded him; mental illness was not part of television's discourse. But when the show went on, Sullivan found Logan backstage looking terrible. Logan told him he regretted not having spoken up about something so meaningful. As quick as he might fire a comedian, Ed ordered the music to stop, and went onstage to say, here's Logan, and this is what Logan said to the camera and the country:

"This has been gratifying to my ego, but it's not important. As it happens, I do have one important thing to tell the country, and I'll tell it quickly. I never got any of the awards I've won until

❝We're really excited that we have on our stage such an outstanding jazzman.**❞**

I'd been committed to a mental hospital and released from it. I tell you this because the world is suffering from tension, with the result that many people are crippled by mental breakdowns. The old way of treating them was to hide them in the garden house when people came to visit in warm weather, or lock them up in the attic in winter. You don't have to do either any more. A lot of people who are disturbed mentally can be cured, just as typhoid, scarlet fever, and tuberculosis can be cured. There is no reason why they should go through life bearing a stigma because they have once been mental patients. The proudest moment of my life is that although I had been in the theater a good many years, I never won the Pulitzer Prize until after I had been in the sanitarium."

There was, of course, a hush, and then the great applause. There are occasions of great privilege, and sometimes we are applauding as much for ourselves as for the occasion, having been surprised that we could be so moved, that there was still enough innocence, generosity, and depth of feeling in us to respond. It's not just that so many thousands of letters and telegrams of approval poured in afterwards, nor that funds suddenly became available in so many states for mental-health programs that had never before been appreciated. After all, advertising agencies don't spend millions of dollars of their clients' money on television commercials without expecting to sell more of the product. Speech modifies behavior, and speech on television, spontaneous and heartfelt, can even sell understanding.

But think also of the discovery of the medium — its powerful intimacy; the close-ups on character. In the theater, at its best, we are spellbound. At the movies, by the direct access of those huge shadows to our subconscious, we are overwhelmed. And most of us have never been to the parties or the nightclubs reported in the gossip columns. But at home, with a suddenly unbuttoned Logan, in the awkwardness and sincerity, we become familiar, and are made to think. Or at least we used to be, before television decided that if it gave us too much time to do so, we'd switch channels. Since Logan, television has almost seemed to specialize in understanding mental illness, as, in fact, it specializes more than any other entertainment medium in exploring social problems from rape to racism. But it has also specialized in intimacy, which is where the talk shows came from. What are all these famous people really like — as it were, demystified — when nobody else has written their words, when they're caught with their emotions showing?

**Overleaf: Ed with
Harpo Marx and
trumpet in 1961.**

Ed talks, in 1955, to John Huston (above) about the director's war experiences, and to suspense-meister Alfred Hitchcock (right) about a television award for "Best Dramatic Series" (*Alfred Hitchcock Presents*) in 1956.

On "Sullivision," for the first time in such intimacy, we could put faces on the voices from radio who would go on to television careers of their own, like Jack Benny, George Burns, Bing Crosby, Jimmy Durante, Bob Hope, Frank Sinatra, and Red Skelton. We attached bodies to voices we'd heard only on the jukebox, like Louis Armstrong, Nat "King" Cole, Ella Fitzgerald, Barbra Streisand, and the Supremes. We met stars of stage like Noël Coward and Laurence Olivier, Helen Hayes and Richard Burton, Marcel Marceau and Rudolf Nureyev. And, to a degree that would have seemed impossible in 1948, we met stars of screen.

Hollywood hated television, before television moved to Hollywood. It was Sullivan's genius to make a deal with Hollywood, to convince studio nawabs like Goldwyn that television was really free publicity; pre-release snippets of forthcoming films — including thirty minutes devoted to *Guys and Dolls* — would entice millions to their neighborhood theaters, to see the whole thing; that actors on a studio stage in Manhattan could promote their careers, and the vehicles of those careers, all over the country without dissipating their magical properties. The consequence for Ed's show was a steady stream of star-power from the likes of Fred Astaire, Humphrey Bogart, James Cagney, Gary Cooper, Olivia de Havilland, Douglas Fairbanks, Errol Flynn, Henry Fonda, Betty Grable, Rita Hayworth, Audrey Hepburn, Charlton Heston, John Huston, Burt Lancaster, Vivien Leigh, Sal Mineo, Robert Mitchum, Paul Newman, Merle Oberon, Gregory Peck, Edward G. Robinson, Ginger Rogers, Mickey Rooney, James Stewart, Elizabeth Taylor, John Wayne, and Orson Welles. And some-

Ed and Walt Disney, off camera, during a 1953 show devoted to "The Walt Disney Story." From playing golf together, they would move on to square off against each other on separate channels at the same time Sunday nights.

Overleaf: A just-starting-out Barbra Streisand, in 1962, sings "Come Back to Me." And a still-going-strong Judy Garland sings "Come Rain or Come Shine" in her first live appearance, in 1965.

times they amazed us, like Charles Laughton reading from the Bible.

Bette Davis was a holdout. Sullivan offered Davis $10,000 to do her Tallulah Bankhead impersonation. Bette refused, explaining: "Miss Bankhead isn't well enough known to warrant my imitating her." And then there was Ingrid Bergman, who had to run away from Hollywood to Europe after her affair with Italian director Roberto Rossellini. On July 18, 1956, Sullivan announced that she would return that fall to be on his show. Twentieth Century-Fox had made the deal, to promote *Anastasia*, but nobody had told Ingrid. She said from London that she had no intention of being on his show. So Sullivan went onstage on July 29 for one of his most embarrassing moments. He asked his audience to decide, for him, whether Bergman's "seven-and-a-half years of penance" had been enough to warrant their absolving her. If so, he'd invite her again. "Ingrid never forgave me," he said later, "and she was right."

Gloria Swanson, however, did show up to tell an astonished nation that she believed in God.

And there isn't room enough to talk about the entertainers Ed turned into stars merely by having them on his show. Just being there with Helen Hayes, Louis Armstrong, Joan Sutherland, and Ted Williams, they were knighted, as if by an electric sword. Celebrity is what a democratic society has instead of aristocrats. When Warhol came along to promise us we'd all be famous for fifteen minutes, he was being naive; it took Ed less time than that to do the trick for an astonishing range of people who will be remembered as long as there is videotape, or Trivial Pursuit.

In what must be one of the most engrossing book excerpts on television, Helen Hayes (above) reads from her memoirs, *On Reflection,* in 1968.

Henry Fonda (left) in 1961, reads Abraham Lincoln's Gettysburg Address.

Judy Holliday, in 1957, sings "I'm Going Back" from *Bells Are Ringing*.

Vivien Leigh, a long way from Tara, does a scene from *Tovarich* in 1963.

66Tonight our stage is crowded with memories, and our show is jammed with stars.99

Celeste Holm, in 1955, sings "I Can't Say No."

Opposite: Celestial bodies Rita Hayworth and Lilli Palmer, offstage, two days before they appeared separately on Ed's stage in 1953.

Frank just dropped by to say hi in 1964 (top), but Bing came to sing. And he did so, eight times, including here in 1956 (above), when he performs "True Love" from Cole Porter's *High Society*. Opposite: Nat "King" Cole in 1950. Although he was on the show many times, singing such hits as "Mona Lisa," "Unforgettable," and "Too Young," Cole quit those Sunday nights for a while when Ed insisted he sing an old hit instead of introducing a new single.

———

Overleaf: Benny Goodman and his fourteen-member band, in 1957, do their classic "Sing, Sing, Sing."

Cab Calloway, in his
color-coordinated
dancing shoes, stops
traffic in 1963 with
"Minnie the Moocher."

Ethel Merman (left), in 1966, does a medley from her hit Broadway show *Annie Get Your Gun.*

Overleaf: When the great clown Lucille Ball cries, Ed laughs. She appeared on the show thirteen times, starting in 1954.

Sophie Tucker shows a grateful nation what the last of the red-hot mamas can do. Here, in 1960, she performs "Being in the Business of Staying Young."

Ed and Louis Armstrong went all over the world together, from Guantánamo in Cuba to Spoleto in Italy. Here's Satchmo in 1961, with Duke Ellington, performing "Nobody Knows the Trouble I've Seen."

Afterword

Looking back, my interest in Ed Sullivan and his show began in our den where the family would gather in front of the television set each Sunday night at eight o'clock. Sullivan's was the only program that our family of four watched together, though we each had our own favorites: My dad loved the sounds of Ella and Satchmo. My mother preferred Broadway actors like Richard Burton and Julie Andrews. My brother and I were drawn to the rock and roll. After all, Elvis, the Beatles, and the Stones had performed live on the Sullivan stage.

We arrived in this country in the Fifties, and *The Ed Sullivan Show* was, in a way, a window into understanding America. The show itself was a melting pot. No other television show ever featured such an awesome array of world-class talent. This achievement will never be repeated. Ed tossed up a great mix — comedy, novelty, ballet, Broadway, and the greatest popular music of the day. Fortunately, Ed's taste was eclectic, his personal stamp indelibly etched on each Sunday night presentation.

During the last few years, as we have been preparing a series of new shows based on the films and tapes of the original programs, I have been struck by how many great performances there are. With this book, as with the television shows and videos, we have tried to recapture some of that magic. *A Really Big Show* is our tactile attempt at the richness and diversity of entertainment that Ed and a galaxy of stars offered us each week for twenty-three years.

Poring through this material I have come to appreciate not only Ed the showman, but Ed the man. More than just a genial emcee, Sullivan was a first-rate producer who changed the face of a newborn medium. To some extent he shaped the way we enjoy and appreciate entertainment today.

Sullivan's passion was the crown jewel in the CBS Sunday night lineup throughout the Fifties and Sixties, but the shows were never rebroadcast. Ensconced in a New Jersey film vault for decades have been some of the most riveting performances in television history.

I first became aware of this library in 1972, just a year after Ed Sullivan had gone off the air. I was working on the documentary feature *Elvis On Tour*, and in the course of my research I screened Elvis's three historic appearances on the show. At the time I never dreamed that one day I would be able to help bring these and other unforgettable moments to millions of viewers around the world.

In a way my Sullivan experience has come full circle. Today I have the pleasure of watching these new shows with *"meu amor"* Claudia and our children, Joshua and Dakota. It's a joy for us to see Josh laughing out loud at Red Skelton or Richard Pryor and being awestruck at the antics of plate-spinner Eric Brenn; and our daughter Cody is already up to speed on Topo Gigio and various early Muppet creations. Thanks to the miracle of celluloid and videotape, these and other performances are as alive today as ever.

Finally, I never would have thought to get involved with the Sullivan show if it hadn't been for my pioneering parents. George and Mimi had the courage to bring us to America, a decision for which I'm eternally grateful.

And Ed, I thank you for the memories, then and now. We hope you're back for good.

—ANDREW SOLT

The following is a selected list of the ten thousand performers
who appeared on *The Ed Sullivan Show* during its twenty-three-year run. The names are arranged
alphabetically, followed by the number of appearances.

HANK AARON, *1*
ABBOTT AND COSTELLO, *1*
DON ADAMS, *5*
EDIE ADAMS, *5*
JOEY ADAMS, *9*
ANNA MARIA ALBERGHETTI, *13*
EDDIE ALBERT, *8*
ROBERT ALDA, *2*
MUHAMMAD ALI, *2*
STEVE ALLEN, *2*
ALLEN AND ROSSI, *17*
WOODY ALLEN, *4*
JUNE ALLYSON, *1*
DON AMECHE, *1*
ED AMES, *7*
NANCY AMES, *9*
THE AMES BROTHERS, *20*
MOREY AMSTERDAM, *6*
EDDIE "ROCHESTER"
    ANDERSON, *1*
JUDITH ANDERSON, *4*
MARIAN ANDERSON, *1*
DANA ANDREWS, *1*
JULIE ANDREWS, *4*
THE ANDREWS SISTERS, *1*
DENYSE ANGE, *1*
THE ANIMALS, *6*
PAUL ANKA, *13*
ANN-MARGRET, *4*
RAY ANTHONY, *1*
EDDIE ARCARO, *5*
EVE ARDEN, *2*
HAROLD ARLEN, *4*
LOUIS ARMSTRONG, *18*
DESI ARNAZ, *8*
JAMES ARNESS, *1*
EDDY ARNOLD, *2*
BEATRICE ARTHUR, *1*
ELIZABETH ASHLEY, *1*
THE ASSOCIATION, *2*
FRED ASTAIRE, *5*
MARY ASTOR, *1*
CHET ATKINS, *3*
TED ATKINSON, *2*
GENE AUTRY, *2*
FRANKIE AVALON, *4*
LAUREN BACALL, *2*
YEN BACH, *1*
PEARL BAILEY, *23*
BIL BAIRD, *13*
CARROLL BAKER, *2*
LAVERN BAKER, *3*
LUCILLE BALL, *13*
CARL BALLANTINE, *8*
KAY BALLANTINE, *5*
MARTIN BALLANTINE, *1*
THE BAND, *1*
TALLULAH BANKHEAD, *1*
ERNIE BANKS, *1*
BRIGITTE BARDOT, *3*
SANDY BARON, *2*
GENE BARRY, *2*

LIONEL BARRYMORE, *1*
JAMES BARTON, *2*
COUNT BASIE, *7*
PEG LEG BATES, *15*
THE BEACH BOYS, *2*
ORSON BEAN, *7*
THE BEATLES, *10*
CLYDE BEATTY, *4*
GILBERT BECAUD, *1*
THE BEE GEES, *1*
BARBARA BEL GEDDES, *1*
HARRY BELAFONTE, *8*
WILLIAM BENDIX, *1*
DAVID BEN-GURION, *1*
TONY BENNETT, *15*
JACK BENNY, *11*
BROOK BENTON, *4*
EDGAR BERGEN, *7*
POLLY BERGEN, *8*
MILTON BERLE, *4*
IRVING BERLIN, *3*
SHELLEY BERMAN, *21*
HERSCHEL BERNARDI, *2*
LEONARD BERNSTEIN, *1*
YOGI BERRA, *6*
KEN BERRY, *1*
LEON BIBB, *9*
THEODORE BIKEL, *3*
ACKER BILK, *4*
JOEY BISHOP, *8*
BILL BLACK COMBO, *2*
CILLA BLACK, *3*
VIVIAN BLAINE, *3*
JANET BLAIR, *8*
EUBIE BLAKE, *1*
BLOOD, SWEAT AND TEARS, *2*
ANN BLYTH, *2*
BOB AND RAY, *5*
HUMPHREY BOGART, *1*
GARY "U.S." BONDS, *1*
PAT BOONE, *4*
RICHARD BOONE, *3*
SHIRLEY BOOTH, *2*
VICTOR BORGE, *24*
JIMMY BOYD, *6*
CHARLES BOYER, *2*
KEN BOYER, *1*
ERIC BRENN, *8*
DAVID BRENNER, *1*
EILEEN BRENNAN, *2*
TERESA BREWER, *31*
LLOYD BRIDGES, *1*
LOU BROCK, *1*
BROOKLYN BRIDGE, *1*
ALBERT BROOKS, *1*
MEL BROOKS, *1*
THE BROTHERS FOUR, *3*
GEORGIA BROWN, *4*
JAMES BROWN, *2*
JOE E. BROWN, *2*
DAVE BRUBECK QUARTET, *1*
HEIDI BRUHL, *1*

ANITA BRYANT, *5*
YUL BRYNNER, *4*
CONRAD BUCKNER, *13*
JULIE BUDD, *3*
CAROL BURNETT, *5*
GEORGE BURNS, *4*
BURNS AND SCHREIBER, *2*
RICHARD BURTON, *3*
DICK BUTTON, *3*
RED BUTTONS, *10*
PAT BUTTRAM, *9*
SPRING BYINGTON, *1*
JOHN BYNER, *17*
THE BYRDS, *1*
SID CAESAR, *15*
JAMES CAGNEY, *4*
CHARLIE CALLAS, *1*
MARIA CALLAS, *1*
CAB CALLOWAY, *11*
GODFREY CAMBRIDGE, *1*
ROY CAMPANELLA, *3*
LANA CANTRELL, *15*
RON CAREY, *4*
GEORGE CARLIN, *11*
KITTY CARLISLE, *1*
JUDY CARNE, *2*
ART CARNEY, *13*
LESLIE CARON, *1*
THE CARPENTERS, *2*
VIKKI CARR, *3*
JOHN CARRADINE, *1*
DIAHANN CARROLL, *9*
JEAN CARROLL, *29*
PAT CARROLL, *2*
JOHNNY CARSON, *6*
JACK CARTER, *49*
JOHNNY CASH, *1*
BILLY CASPER, JR., *1*
HOPALONG CASSIDY, *1*
JACK CASSIDY, *3*
ROY CASTLE, *3*
FIDEL CASTRO, *1*
DICK CAVETT, *1*
FLORENCE CHADWICK, *1*
WILT CHAMBERLAIN, *1*
THE CHAMBERS BROTHERS, *3*
MARGE AND GOWER
    CHAMPION, *5*
THE CHAMPS, *1*
CAROL CHANNING, *8*
CYD CHARISSE, *5*
RAY CHARLES, *2*
CHARO, *2*
PADDY CHAYEFSKY, *1*
CHUBBY CHECKER, *2*
CHECKMATES, LTD., *1*
MAURICE CHEVALIER, *9*
DANE CLARK, *1*
DAVE CLARK FIVE, *12*
FRED CLARK, *1*
PETULA CLARK, *11*
ROY CLARK, *3*

JAN CLAYTON, *1*
VAN CLIBURN, *2*
MONTGOMERY CLIFT, *1*
ROSEMARY CLOONEY, *16*
IMOGENE COCA, *4*
JOE COCKER AND THE
    GREASEBAND, *1*
GEORGE M. COHAN, *2*
MYRON COHEN, *43*
NAT "KING" COLE, *13*
DOROTHY COLLINS, *3*
JOAN COLLINS, *1*
JERRY COLONNA, *1*
BETTY COMDEN, *2*
PERRY COMO, *2*
CHRIS CONNER, *2*
SEAN CONNERY, *1*
BOB CONSIDINE, *1*
BARBARA COOK, *2*
SAM COOKE, *2*
GARY COOPER, *3*
KEVIN CORCORAN, *1*
FRANCO CORELLI, *7*
JILL COREY, *4*
BILL COSBY, *1*
LOU COSTELLO, *4*
BOB COUSY, *1*
NOËL COWARD, *2*
THE COWSILLS, *2*
WALLY COX, *3*
JEANNE CRAIN, *2*
BRODERICK CRAWFORD, *1*
CREEDENCE CLEARWATER
    REVIVAL, *2*
THE CREW CUTS, *1*
HUME CRONYN, *4*
BING CROSBY, *5*
BOB CROSBY, *2*
GARY CROSBY, *1*
NORM CROSBY, *14*
XAVIER CUGAT, *16*
TONY CURTIS, *2*
DAN DAILEY, *2*
SALVADOR DALI, *1*
JACQUES D'AMBOISE, *3*
DAMITA JO, *2*
VIC DAMONE, *6*
BILL DANA, *17*
DOROTHY DANDRIDGE, *6*
RODNEY DANGERFIELD, *15*
DENISE DARCEL, *1*
BOBBY DARIN, *6*
JAMES DARREN, *1*
JOHN DAVIDSON, *3*
CHARLES DAVIS, *7*
SAMMY DAVIS, JR., *8*
DENNIS DAY, *1*
GLORIA DE HAVEN, *5*
OLIVIA DE HAVILLAND, *2*
AGNES DEMILLE, *1*
JACKIE DESHANNON, *1*
BRANDON DE WILDE, *2*

BILLY DE WOLFE, *10*
JAMES DEAN, *1*
JIMMY DEAN, *3*
JACK DEMPSEY, *6*
COLLEEN DEWHURST, *1*
NEIL DIAMOND, *1*
BO DIDDLEY, *1*
PHYLLIS DILLER, *6*
DION DIMUCCI, *1*
DINO, DESI AND BILLY, *1*
WALT DISNEY, *2*
FATS DOMINO, *2*
THE DOODLETOWN PIPERS, *5*
THE DOORS, *1*
TOMMY DORSEY, *2*
KIRK DOUGLAS, *4*
MELVYN DOUGLAS, *2*
MIKE DOUGLAS, *3*
ARNOLD DOVER, *1*
MORTON DOWNEY, *1*
ALFRED DRAKE, *4*
PAUL DRAKE, *1*
DON DRYSDALE, *1*
PETER DUCHIN, *2*
HOWARD DUFF, *1*
PATTY DUKE, *1*
JIMMY DURANTE, *9*
NANCY DUSSAULT, *5*
CLINT EASTWOOD, *2*
BILLY ECKSTINE, *9*
NELSON EDDY, *3*
BARBARA EDEN, *1*
ANDRÉ EGLEVSKY, *3*
DWIGHT D. EISENHOWER, *1*
DUKE ELLINGTON, *10*
MAURICE EVANS, *3*
NORMAN EVANS, *4*
THE EVERLY BROTHERS, *9*
FABIAN, *2*
NANETTE FABRAY, *6*
SAMMY FAIN, *1*
DOUGLAS FAIRBANKS, JR., *6*
LOLA FALANA, *1*
JINX FALKENBURG, *1*
FRANCES FARMER, *2*
EILEEN FARRELL, *4*
FRANK FAY, *1*
JOSÉ FELICIANO, *1*
NORMAN FELL, *1*
FERRANTE AND TEICHER, *3*
JOSÉ FERRER, *3*
ARTHUR FIEDLER, *1*
GRACIE FIELDS, *8*
TOTIE FIELDS, *20*
THE FIFTH DIMENSION, *8*
FINNISH WOMEN GYMNASTS, *1*
FIRST EDITION, *1*
EDDIE FISHER, *10*
BARRY FITZGERALD, *2*
ELLA FITZGERALD, *8*
THE FLEETWOODS, *1*
RHONDA FLEMING, *1*
ERROL FLYNN, *2*
HENRY FONDA, *6*
FRANK FONTAINE, *7*
LYNN FONTANNE, *2*
MARGOT FONTEYN, *4*
CONSTANCE FORD, *1*
GERALD FORD, *1*
GLENN FORD, *1*
MARY FORD, *4*
WHITEY FORD, *7*

HELEN FORREST, *3*
JOHN FORSYTHE, *4*
PHIL FOSTER, *9*
THE FOUR ACES, *4*
THE FOUR COINS, *1*
THE FOUR LADS, *3*
THE FOUR PREPS, *2*
THE FOUR SEASONS, *3*
THE FOUR TOPS, *4*
SERGIO FRANCHI, *24*
TONY FRANCIOSA, *1*
ARLENE FRANCIS, *1*
CONNIE FRANCIS, *26*
WILLIAM FRAWLEY, *2*
JOE FRAZIER, *1*
STAN FREBERG, *2*
FREDDIE AND THE DREAMERS, *1*
ALBERT FREEMAN, JR., *1*
DON FREEMAN, *2*
THE FRIENDS OF DISTINCTION, *1*
RUDOLF FRIML, *3*
JANE FROMAN, *6*
DAVID FROST, *1*
DAVID FRYE, *11*
ANNETTE FUNICELLO, *1*
ALLEN FUNT, *1*
CLARK GABLE, *3*
HELEN GALLAGHER, *4*
RITA GAM, *1*
JOE GARAGIOLA, *1*
REGINALD GARDINER, *3*
JUDY GARLAND, *2*
ERROLL GARNER, *4*
PEGGY ANN GARNER, *1*
JOHN GARY, *1*
MARVIN GAYE, *1*
MITZI GAYNOR, *3*
BOBBIE GENTRY, *5*
GERRY AND THE PACEMAKERS, *4*
IRA GERSHWIN, *1*
GEORGIA GIBBS, *6*
ALTHEA GIBSON, *4*
BOB GIBSON, *3*
JOHN GIELGUD, *1*
FRANK GIFFORD, *1*
ASTRUD GILBERTO, *1*
JACK GILFORD, *1*
DIZZY GILLESPIE, *1*
ANITA GILLETTE, *3*
HERMIONE GINGOLD, *8*
LILLIAN GISH, *1*
JACKIE GLEASON, *9*
GEORGE GOBEL, *5*
PAULETTE GODDARD, *2*
ARTHUR GODFREY, *4*
BOBBY GOLDSBORO, *1*
RUBY GOLDSTEIN, *2*
BENNY GOODMAN, *5*
DODY GOODMAN, *4*
GALE GORDON, *2*
RUTH GORDON, *1*
LESLEY GORE, *4*
EYDIE GORME, *9*
FRANK GORSHIN, *12*
ROBERT GOULET, *15*
HARRY GOZ, *1*
BETTY GRABLE, *1*
FARLEY GRANGER, *1*
CARY GRANT, *1*
GOGI GRANT, *1*
THE GRASS ROOTS, *1*
PETER GRAVES, *1*

TERESA GRAVES, *1*
BILLY GRAY, *1*
DOLORES GRAY, *1*
KATHRYN GRAYSON, *1*
BUDDY GRECO, *6*
ADOLPH GREEN, *3*
SHECKY GREENE, *6*
DICK GREGORY, *1*
JOEL GREY, *2*
VIRGINIA GREY, *2*
MERV GRIFFIN, *1*
ANDY GRIFFITH, *3*
TAMMY GRIMES, *4*
GEORGE GRIZZARD, *1*
DICK GROAT, *1*
ALEC GUINNESS, *1*
BUDDY HACKETT, *2*
BILL HALEY AND HIS COMETS, *2*
JACK HALEY, *2*
JUANITA HALL, *6*
GEORGE HAMILTON, *4*
ROY HAMILTON, *1*
OSCAR HAMMERSTEIN II, *6*
LIONEL HAMPTON, *6*
W.C. HANDY, *6*
CAROL HANEY, *14*
CEDRIC HARDWICKE, *2*
THE HARLEM GLOBETROTTERS, *6*
PAT HARRINGTON, *1*
JULIE HARRIS, *4*
PHIL HARRIS, *1*
RICHARD HARRIS, *1*
NOEL HARRISON, *3*
REX HARRISON, *6*
BILLY HARTACK, *2*
THE HARVEST MOON
  DANCERS, *21*
LAURENCE HARVEY, *1*
RICHIE HAVENS, *2*
JUNE HAVER, *1*
JUNE HAVOC, *1*
HELEN HAYES, *7*
PETER LIND HAYES, *8*
RICHARD HAYMAN, *1*
DICK HAYMES, *2*
LELAND HAYWARD, *2*
RITA HAYWORTH, *2*
LEE HAZLEWOOD, *4*
RICHARD HEARNE, *23*
EILEEN HECKART, *2*
VAN HEFLIN, *3*
DAVID HEMMINGS, *2*
FLORENCE HENDERSON, *6*
SKITCH HENDERSON, *1*
SONJA HENIE, *1*
AUDREY HEPBURN, *2*
JERRY HERMAN, *2*
WOODY HERMAN, *9*
HERMAN'S HERMITS, *3*
CHARLTON HESTON, *6*
THE HIGHWAYMEN, *3*
ARTHUR HILL, *1*
CONRAD HILTON, *1*
HINES, HINES AND BROWN, *2*
JEROME HINES, *1*
AL HIRT, *14*
GIL HODGES, *3*
JOHN HODIAK, *1*
BEN HOGAN, *4*
HAL HOLBROOK, *3*
WILLIAM HOLDEN, *1*
HOLIDAY ON ICE, *3*

JUDY HOLLIDAY, *1*
STANLEY HOLLOWAY, *1*
BUDDY HOLLY AND THE
  CRICKETS, *2*
CELESTE HOLM, *5*
LOU HOLTZ, *2*
BOB HOPE, *4*
MARY HOPKIN, *2*
LENA HORNE, *4*
MARILYN HORNE, *1*
EDWARD EVERETT HORTON, *1*
JOHNNY HORTON, *2*
ELSTON HOWARD, *5*
SALLY ANN HOWES, *4*
ENGLEBERT HUMPERDINCK, *2*
HUNGARIAN OLYMPIC TEAM, *1*
FERLIN HUSKEY, *1*
JOHN HUSTON, *4*
FRANK IFIELD, *4*
THE INK SPOTS, *4*
BURL IVES, *3*
MAHALIA JACKSON, *6*
THE JACKSON 5, *2*
LOU JACOBI, *1*
HARRY JAMES, *9*
SONNY JAMES, *6*
TOMMY JAMES AND THE
  SHONDELLS, *2*
JEFFERSON AIRPLANE, *1*
ANNE JEFFREYS, *2*
FRAN JEFFRIES, *4*
GEORGE JESSEL, *3*
JOFFREY BALLET, *1*
INGEMAR JOHANSSON, *2*
ARTE JOHNSON, *1*
VAN JOHNSON, *4*
JOHNNY JOHNSTON, *3*
DEAN JONES, *1*
JACK JONES, *5*
JAMES EARL JONES, *1*
SHIRLEY JONES, *2*
SPIKE JONES, *1*
TOM JONES, *7*
JANIS JOPLIN, *1*
WILL JORDAN, *13*
DUKE KAHANAMOKU, *1*
KITTY KALLEN, *4*
HELEN KANE, *4*
JACKIE KANNON, *6*
DANNY KAYE, *2*
STUBBY KAYE, *1*
LAINIE KAZAN, *5*
BUSTER KEATON, *6*
-HOWARD KEEL, *1*
EMMETT KELLY, *7*
GENE KELLY, *5*
GRACE KELLY, *3*
PERT KELTON, *3*
STAN KENTON, *1*
LARRY KERT, *1*
THE KESSLER TWINS, *16*
RICHARD KILEY, *4*
THE KIM SISTERS, *25*
ROSLYN KIND, *3*
ALAN KING, *37*
B.B. KING, *1*
CORETTA SCOTT KING, *1*
THE KING FAMILY, *3*
GEORGE KIRBY, *20*
LISA KIRK, *8*
RAHSAAN ROLAND KIRK, *1*
JOE KIRKWOOD, *1*

Dorothy Kirsten, 3
Eartha Kitt, 15
Robert Klein, 6
Gladys Knight and the Pips, 4
Buddy Knox, 2
John Kokoman, 1
André Kostelanetz, 2
Ernie Kovacs, 2
Billy J. Kramer and the
    Dakotas, 2
Sid Krofft, 2
Gene Krupa, 3
Bert Lahr, 17
Frankie Laine, 12
Arthur Lake, 1
Hedy Lamarr, 1
Dorothy Lamour, 2
Burt Lancaster, 7
Abbe Lane, 6
Hope Lange, 1
Mario Lanza, 1
Julius La Rosa, 17
Charles Laughton, 6
Carol Lawrence, 17
Gertrude Lawrence, 4
Steve Lawrence, 12
Rickie Layne, 39
Brenda Lee, 4
Kathryn Lee, 5
Michele Lee, 3
Peggy Lee, 13
Pinky Lee, 8
Vivien Leigh, 1
Jack Lemmon, 3
The Lennon Sisters, 4
Jack E. Leonard, 16
Alan Jay Lerner, 5
The Lettermen, 2
Sam Levene, 3
Sam Levenson, 7
Gary Lewis and the Playboys, 5
Jerry Lewis, 8
Jerry Lee Lewis, 1
Joe E. Lewis, 14
Monica Lewis, 5
Robert Q. Lewis, 1
Shari Lewis, 5
Ted Lewis, 10
Liberace, 6
Beatrice Lillie, 4
The Limeliters, 3
Hal Linden, 1
Viveca Lindfors, 1
John Lindsay, 1
Eugene List, 2
Sonny Liston, 2
Little Anthony and the
    Imperials, 2
Rich Little, 5
Harold Lloyd, Jr., 1
Frederick Loewe, 3
Joshua Logan, 3
Lohman and Barkley, 1
Gina Lollobrigida, 3
Guy Lombardo, 5
Julie London, 1
Trini Lopez, 2
Vincent Lopez, 6
Sophia Loren, 5
Peter Lorre, 1
Dorothy Loudon, 4
Joe Louis, 1
Tina Louise, 1

Lovin' Spoonful, 3
Lulu, 1
Alfred Lunt, 2
Ida Lupino, 1
Frankie Lymon, 3
Paul Lynde, 4
Loretta Lynn, 2
Moms Mabley, 4
Jeanette MacDonald, 2
Ali MacGraw, 1
Ted Mack, 1
Gisele MacKenzie, 2
Fred MacMurray, 1
Gordon MacRae, 15
Sheila MacRae, 4
Sal Maglie, 3
Anna Magnani, 1
Natalia Makarova, 1
Miriam Makeba, 3
The Mamas and the Papas, 3
Henry Mancini, 1
Jayne Mansfield, 2
Mickey Mantle, 12
Marcel Marceau, 3
Fredric March, 1
Hal March, 4
Rocky Marciano, 8
Roger Maris, 5
Dewey "Pigmeat" Markham, 21
Guy Marks, 12
Marian Marlowe, 19
E.G. Marshall, 1
Jay Marshall, 8
Martha and the Vandellas, 1
Dean Martin, 1
Tony Martin, 12
Wink Martindale, 1
Lee Marvin, 1
Harpo Marx, 2
Jackie Mason, 20
James and Pamela Mason, 3
Raymond Massey, 2
Eddie Mathews, 1
Johnny Mathis, 13
Peter Max, 1
Willie Mays, 7
Patricia McBride, 7
Mercedes McCambridge, 2
Paul McCartney, 1
Tim McCarver, 1
Patty McCormack, 1
Ruth McDevitt, 3
Gil McDougald, 3
Roddy McDowall, 2
Darren McGavin, 1
Barry McGuire, 1
Biff McGuire, 1
The McGuire Sisters, 22
Rod McKuen, 1
Denny McLain, 1
Barbara McNair, 7
Carmen McRae, 2
Vaughn Meader, 4
Audrey Meadows, 2
Kay Medford, 2
Ralph Meeker, 4
Melanie, 2
Lauritz Melchior, 4
James Melton, 4
GianCarlo Menotti, 2
Yehudi Menuhin, 3
Melina Mercouri, 2
Ethel Merman, 8

Gary Merrill, 1
Robert Merrill, 17
Cary Middlecoff, 1
Ray Middleton, 3
Ray Milland, 2
Ann Miller, 2
Glenn Miller, 2
Mrs. Miller, 2
The Mills Brothers, 3
Sal Mineo, 6
Liza Minnelli, 11
Carmen Miranda, 1
Chad Mitchell Trio, 3
Guy Mitchell, 6
Scoey Mitchlll, 8
Robert Mitchum, 4
Ron Mix, 1
Johnny Mize, 3
Domenico Modugno, 3
Anna Moffo, 6
Moiseyev Dance Troupe, 1
Corbett Monica, 10
Matt Monro, 3
Vaughn Monroe, 10
Ricardo Montalban, 1
Robert Montgomery, 1
Garry Moore, 1
Melba Moore, 2
Victor Moore, 4
Rita Moreno, 1
Jane Morgan. 24
Jaye P. Morgan, 3
Patricia Morison, 2
Greg Morris, 1
Karen Morrow, 1
Gary Morton, 2
Willie Mosconi, 3
Zero Mostel, 1
Edward Mulhare, 2
Patrice Munsel, 1
The Muppets, 25
Don Murray, 1
Jan Murray, 14
Kathryn and Arthur
    Murray, 1
Ken Murray, 5
Edward R. Murrow, 3
Stan Musial, 2
Bess Myerson, 1
Jim Nabors, 1
Clarence Nash, 1
Ogden Nash, 1
Maria Neglia, 12
Byron Nelson, 5
Ricky Nelson, 1
Peter Nero, 9
Don Newcombe, 2
Bob Newhart, 8
Anthony Newley, 4
Paul Newman, 3
Phyllis Newman, 1
Wayne Newton, 7
Leslie Nielsen, 1
Birgit Nilsson, 6
David Niven, 1
Richard M. Nixon, 1
Jay North, 1
Sheree North, 1
Kim Novak, 1
Rudolf Nureyev, 2
Louis Nye, 3
Merle Oberon, 1
Hugh O'Brian, 2

Margaret O'Brien, 2
Pat O'Brien, 6
Donald O'Connor, 2
Odetta, 1
Maureen O'Hara, 3
Laurence Olivier, 1
Jerry Orbach, 1
Roy Orbison, 1
Tessie O'Shea, 5
Peter O'Toole, 1
Buck Owens, 3
Jesse Owens, 2
Jack Paar, 7
Patti Page, 18
Janis Paige, 2
Jack Palance, 1
Arnold Palmer, 1
Betsy Palmer, 3
Lilli Palmer, 6
Peter Palmer, 6
Fess Parker, 1
Michael Parks, 1
Patachou, 12
Floyd Patterson, 2
Les Paul, 4
Freda Payne, 1
Minnie Pearl, 2
Gregory Peck, 4
Jan Peerce, 11
Anthony Perkins, 1
John Perkins, 1
Itzhak Perlman, 4
Peter and Gordon, 1
Bernadette Peters, 1
Roberta Peters, 41
Edith Piaf, 8
Marguerite Piazza, 1
Walter Pidgeon, 3
Billie Pierce, 1
Jimmy Piersall, 1
Ezio Pinza, 2
The Platters, 6
Gary Player, 1
Suzanne Pleshette, 1
Maya Plisetskaya, 1
Milt Plum, 1
Christopher Plummer, 1
Lily Pons, 5
Cole Porter. 2
Tom Poston, 1
Dick Powell, 1
Jane Powell, 4
Perez Prado, 1
Otto Preminger, 1
Elvis Presley, 3
Harve Presnell, 1
Robert Preston, 1
Gilbert Price, 3
Leontyne Price, 2
Lloyd Price, 1
Vincent Price, 3
Louis Prima, 8
Professor Backwards, 15
Juliet Prowse, 7
Richard Pryor, 13
Gary Puckett and the
    Union Gap, 4
Anthony Quinn, 1
Charlotte Rae, 6
George Raft, 2
John Raitt, 7
Boots Randolph, 1
Rare Earth, 1

LOU RAWLS, 3
JOHNNIE RAY, 8
GENE RAYMOND, 1
THE RAYS, 2
RONALD REAGAN, 1
MICHAEL REDGRAVE, 1
DELLA REESE, 17
PHIL REGAN, 2
CHARLES NELSON REILLY, 6
CARL REINER, 1
PAUL REVERE AND THE
    RAIDERS, 1
ALLIE REYNOLDS, 1
DEBBIE REYNOLDS, 2
JAMES "DUSTY" RHODES, 1
BUDDY RICH, 2
CLIFF RICHARD, 3
MAURICE "ROCKET"
    RICHARD, 1
PAUL RICHARDS, 1
RICHIARDI, 14
HARRY RICHMAN, 3
THE RIGHTEOUS BROTHERS, 1
JEANNIE C. RILEY, 3
CYRIL RITCHARD, 2
CHITA RIVERA, 2
JOAN RIVERS, 20
JOHNNY RIVERS, 1
PHIL RIZZUTO, 3
JASON ROBARDS, JR., 3
JEROME ROBBINS, 2
PERNELL ROBERTS, 1
TONY ROBERTS, 1
BILL "BOJANGLES" ROBINSON, 1
EDWARD G. ROBINSON, 2
FRANK ROBINSON, 1
JACKIE ROBINSON, 2
SMOKEY ROBINSON AND THE
    MIRACLES, 2
SUGAR RAY ROBINSON, 7
FLORA ROBSON, 1
MRS. KNUTE ROCKNE, 3
JIMMIE RODGERS, 4
RICHARD RODGERS, 14
CHI CHI RODRIGUEZ, 1
TOMMY ROE, 1
GINGER ROGERS, 2
ROY ROGERS AND DALE EVANS, 2
WILL ROGERS, JR., 1
THE ROLLING STONES, 6
HAROLD ROME, 1
MICKEY ROONEY, 6
ELEANOR ROOSEVELT, 2
ROSE MARIE, 1
STEVE ROSSI, 2
ROWAN AND MARTIN, 15
GENA ROWLANDS, 1
BILLY JOE ROYAL, 1
JANE RUSSELL, 3
NIPSEY RUSSELL, 7
ROSALIND RUSSELL, 1
BABE RUTH, 1
PEGGY RYAN, 2
BOBBY RYDELL, 2
STAFF SGT. BARRY SADLER, 1
MORT SAHL, 5
SOUPY SALES, 4
SAM AND DAVE, 2
SAM THE SHAM AND THE
    PHARAOHS, 1
CARL SANDBURG, 3
GEORGE SANDERS, 1
SANDLER AND YOUNG, 8

TOMMY SANDS, 3
SANTANA, 1
WILLIAM SAROYAN, 1
MARIA SCHELL, 2
MAXIMILIAN SCHELL, 1
ELISABETH SCHWARZKOPF, 1
ALBERT SCHWEITZER, 1
MARTHA SCOTT, 2
THE SEARCHERS, 1
JEAN SEBERG, 4
HARRY SECOMBE, 2
NEIL SEDAKA, 3
THE SEEKERS, 5
BLOSSOM SEELEY, 14
ANDRÉS SEGOVIA, 4
DAVID SEVILLE, 6
RAVI SHANKAR, 1
BOBBY SHANTZ, 1
OMAR SHARIF, 1
WILLIAM SHATNER, 2
MICKEY SHAUGHNESSY, 2
ROBERT SHAW, 2
DICK SHAWN, 9
MOIRA SHEARER, 2
GEORGE SHEARING, 3
ALLAN SHERMAN, 5
BOBBY SHERMAN, 1
ROBERT SHERWOOD, 2
ROBERTA SHERWOOD, 4
DINAH SHORE, 3
CESARE SIEPI, 9
BEVERLY SILLS, 1
PHIL SILVERS, 15
SIMON AND GARFUNKEL, 1
NINA SIMONE, 1
FRANK SINATRA, 3
FRANK SINATRA, JR., 2
NANCY SINATRA, 11
SISTER SOURIRE
    (THE SINGING NUN), 1
RED SKELTON, 11
SKILES AND HENDERSON, 5
CORNELIA OTIS SKINNER, 4
BILL SKOWRON, 4
ENOS SLAUGHTER, 1
WALTER SLEZAK, 2
SLY AND THE FAMILY STONE, 2
SMITH AND DALE, 21
KATE SMITH, 20
KEELY SMITH, 5
O.C. SMITH, 1
THE SMOTHERS BROTHERS, 2
SAM SNEAD, 5
DUKE SNIDER, 1
SONNY AND CHER, 1
JOE SOUTH, 1
WARREN SPAHN, 3
SPANKY AND OUR GANG, 4
DUSTY SPRINGFIELD, 3
ARNOLD STANG, 6
EDDIE STANKY, 1
KIM STANLEY, 1
KAY STARR, 2
ROGER STAUBACH, 1
TOMMY STEELE, 1
ROD STEIGER, 3
DAVID STEINBERG, 1
STEPPENWOLF, 1
APRIL STEVENS, 1
CONNIE STEVENS, 6
KAYE STEVENS, 6
RISË STEVENS, 15
JAMES STEWART, 3

MARTHA STEWART, 2
STILLER AND MEARA, 36
HAROLD J. STONE, 1
LARRY STORCH, 5
SUSAN STRASBERG, 2
ROBERT STRAUSS, 1
BARBRA STREISAND, 5
ELAINE STRITCH, 2
ENZO STUARTI, 6
JULE STYNE, 4
FRANCIS L. SULLIVAN, 1
THE SUPREMES, 15
JOAN SUTHERLAND, 6
PAT SUZUKI, 3
GLORIA SWANSON, 4
RON SWOBODA, 1
JESSICA TANDY, 4
FRAN TARKENTON, 1
ELIZABETH TAYLOR, 1
JAMES CHARLES TAYLOR, 1
JUNE TAYLOR, 2
RIP TAYLOR, 7
ROBERT TAYLOR, 2
RENATA TEBALDI, 2
THE TEMPTATIONS, 6
RALPH TERRY, 1
PHYLLIS THAXTER, 1
BLANCHE THEBOM, 2
B.J. THOMAS, 2
DANNY THOMAS, 6
JAMES THORPE, 1
THE THREE DEGREES, 1
THE THREE STOOGES, 4
THE TIJUANA BRASS, 3
TINY TIM, 5
Y.A. TITTLE, 3
MICHAEL TODD, JR., 1
MICHAEL TOLAN, 1
FRANCHOT TONE, 1
TOPO GIGIO, 50
MEL TORME, 2
CONSTANCE TOWERS, 3
HELEN TRAUBEL, 3
PIE TRAYNOR, 1
ARTHUR TREACHER, 1
MARGARET TRUMAN, 3
FORREST TUCKER, 1
RICHARD TUCKER, 6
SOPHIE TUCKER, 15
SONNY TUFTS, 1
BOB TURLEY, 1
IKE AND TINA TURNER, 1
LANA TURNER, 1
THE TURTLES, 2
LESLIE UGGAMS, 10
MIYOSHI UMEKI, 2
JOHNNY UNITAS, 1
JERRY VALE, 15
CATERINA VALENTE, 3
KAREN VALENTINE, 2
ANGEL VALENZUELA, 1
RUDY VALLEE, 6
JUNE VALLI, 3
BOBBY VAN, 3
DICK VAN DYKE, 4
JERRY VAN DYKE, 2
MONIQUE VAN VOOREN, 1
VIVIAN VANCE, 2
VANILLA FUDGE, 2
FRANKIE VAUGHAN, 1
SARAH VAUGHAN, 8
KEN VENTURI, 4
GWEN VERDON, 7

JACKIE VERNON, 15
SHIRLEY VERRETT, 4
THE VIENNA BOYS CHOIR, 1
EDWARD VILLELLA, 8
GENE VINCENT AND THE
    BLUECAPS, 1
BOBBY VINTON, 10
BETSY VON FURSTENBERG, 1
ROBERT WAGNER, 1
JIMMY WAKELY, 1
NANCY WALKER, 19
ELI WALLACH, 1
SHANI WALLIS, 2
RAY WALSTON, 2
JESSICA WALTER, 1
BILLY WARD AND THE
    DOMINOES, 2
CLARA WARD, 2
JACK WARDEN, 1
FRED WARING, 2
LEONARD WARREN, 3
LESLEY ANN WARREN, 1
DIONNE WARWICK, 5
ETHEL WATERS, 2
DAVID WAYNE, 4
JOHN WAYNE, 1
WAYNE AND SHUSTER, 58
DENNIS WEAVER, 1
FRITZ WEAVER, 1
JACK WEBB, 2
ROBERT WEEDE, 1
JOHNNY WEISSMULLER, 1
ORSON WELLES, 4
SEÑOR WENCES, 23
BERT WHEELER, 2
GEORGE WHITE, 2
PAUL WHITEMAN, 1
MARGARET WHITING, 3
BILLY WILDER, 1
FRED WILLARD, 4
ESTHER WILLIAMS, 4
HANK WILLIAMS, JR., 2
JOE WILLIAMS, 1
MASON WILLIAMS, 3
ROGER WILLIAMS, 14
TED WILLIAMS, 6
TENNESSEE WILLIAMS, 1
EARL WILSON, 1
FLIP WILSON, 12
JACKIE WILSON, 7
JULIE WILSON, 8
MARIE WILSON, 4
NANCY WILSON, 2
PAUL WINCHELL, 3
SHELLEY WINTERS, 2
STEVIE WONDER, 2
JOANNE WOODWARD, 1
SHEB WOOLEY, 1
JOANNE WORLEY, 2
MICKEY WRIGHT, 1
GRETCHEN WYLER, 1
EARLY WYNN, 1
ED WYNN, 5
GLENN YARBROUGH, 4
CARL YASTRZEMSKI, 1
GIG YOUNG, 1
ROBERT YOUNG, 1
ROLAND YOUNG, 1
THE YOUNG RASCALS, 4
HENNY YOUNGMAN, 14
TIMI YURO, 2
BABE DIDRIKSON ZAHARIAS, 3
DARRYL F. ZANUCK, 2

ACKNOWLEDGMENTS

We are grateful to John Leonard for his thoroughly researched, insightful text; Sarah Lazin, for her follow-through and perfectionism; and Lloyd Ziff for his fine design work. Working with multitalented editor Marianne Partridge has been a particular pleasure, as well as an enjoyable learning experience. We also appreciate the support of Michael Fragnito and Barbara Williams at Viking Studio Books.

A number of key people helped in the very beginning of the Ed Sullivan project, enabling us to get to this stage with a book in hand: Tom McGuire, Tom Hansen, Steven Pollock, Ronald Greenberg, Marcy Levine, Marty Michael, Bob Crestani, Sam Haskell, Greg Lipstone, Ken Coopman, Susan Vaswani, Ray Gross, Bob Steinberg, Daryl Jamison, Bill Steele, Jack Egan, Rafael Pastor, and John Solt.

We also wish to thank Elizabeth Sullivan Precht and Robert Precht, who entrusted this cultural treasure to us and have been very supportive of our efforts to reintroduce Ed Sullivan and his great show to the public.

We are indebted to the following Sullivan show performers for granting us interviews. On tape: Susan Abramson, Carl Ballantine, Conrad Buckner, Vince Calandra, Emily Cole, Barbara Gallagher, Marilyn Gardner, Mary Lynn Gottfried, Will Jordan, Rickie Layne, Vaughn Meader, Hector Peiro, Russ Petranto, Channing Pollock, Marvin Roy, and Lee Truesdell. On camera: Steve Allen, David Crosby, Phyllis Diller, Ella Fitzgerald, Alan King, Carol Lawrence, Rich Little, Ray Manzarek, Jackie Mason, Johnny Mathis, Michelle Phillips, Joan Rivers, Gwen Verdon, and Señor Wences. We very much appreciate the time they gave us and their reflections on Ed, the show, and their involvement with it.

Special mention must be made of the remarkable work of producers Marlo Lewis and Robert Precht and directors Tim Kiley, John Wray, John Moffitt, Bob Schwarz, and Jack Haley, Jr. Their talent, blended with Ed's, gave rise to 1,087 Sunday night shows.

The army of capable people who assisted us in our office in Los Angeles includes Greg Vines, Susan Walker, Tim Tobin, Bennett Crocker, Jeff Gold, Marc Sachnoff, Lori Kleban, Christine Lenihan, Melody Siroty, Kris Hansen-Cascone, Leslie Tong, Scott Cruchley, and Debra Sanderson. In New York at Sarah Lazin Books assistance was lent by Laura Nolan, Holly George-Warren, Alison Kalfus, Devon Jackson, Kymberly Nantz, Tom Nawrocki, Dan Kantor, and Ed Sturmer. The New York Public Library telephone reference department was an invaluable resource.

We especially thank our friends at CBS. From the dawn of television, CBS's visionary chief, William Paley, was always in Ed's corner. Today we are grateful to CBS's current team — Howard Stringer, Jeff Sagansky, Peter Tortorici, Steven Warner, Suzan Mischer, George Schwietzer, Susan Tick, Susan Holliday, Layne Britton, Gordon "Chip" Wood, and especially Marty Silverstein in the photo archives at "Black Rock." We are indebted to the many talented photographers who gave their Sundays to capture these invaluable frames of Sullivan's rehearsals and live broadcasts.

Finally, one of the motivations in doing *A Really Big Show* was for us to work together on a project of this nature. That process has been a pleasure.

— CLAUDIA FALKENBURG AND ANDREW SOLT

PHOTOGRAPHY CREDITS

Most of the photographs in this book were commissioned by and remain the property of CBS photography and are used with permission. We are grateful to the following CBS photographers for their work: Al Candido, Lennie Lautenberger, Irv Haberman, Gaby Rona, Emil Romano, Bob Stahman, William F. Warnecke, Jerry Fitzgerald, and Jerry Urgo.

Other photographs were provided by the following sources: Petrified Films, Inc.: p.6, p.22, p.50. Archive Photos: front endpaper, p.23. UPI/Bettmann: p.24, p.36, p.37 top right, p.37 bottom left, p.165. *Esquire* magazine: © 1965 The Hearst Corporation, all rights reserved: p.44 left. American Stock Photography: p.84, p.110, p.132, p.150, p.164, p.180, p.220. Springer/Bettmann: p.221 top.

ABOUT THE AUTHORS

ANDREW SOLT is a documentary producer/director specializing in entertainment subjects. Born in England, Solt has produced television and feature films on The Rolling Stones, Marilyn Monroe, *The Honeymooners*, Elvis Presley, and the Muppets among others; he was the producer/director of the film, and coauthor of the book, *Imagine: John Lennon*. In 1991, Solt produced two television specials featuring highlights from *The Ed Sullivan Show*.

CLAUDIA FALKENBURG was born in Brazil and earned a graduate degree in biological anthropology from U.C.L.A. This is her first book. Falkenburg and her husband, Andrew Solt, have two children and live in Los Angeles and Santa Ynez, California.

JOHN LEONARD is television critic for *New York* magazine, columnist for *New York Newsday*, book critic for National Public Radio's *Fresh Air*, fiction critic for *The Nation*, and media critic for *CBS Sunday Morning with Charles Kuralt*. Associated with *The New York Times* for fifteen years, he is the author of seven novels and two collections of essays, and has written articles and reviews for publications such as *The Atlantic*, *Harper's*, *Playboy*, *Esquire*, *Vanity Fair*, and *T.V. Guide*.